THE NOT-ENOUGH WIFE

THE *NOT-*ENOUGH WIFE

Why We Look
Outside Ourselves
& How to Stop

JOLENE
WINN

HOUNDSTOOTH
PRESS

THE NOT-ENOUGH WIFE
Why We Look Outside Ourselves & How to Stop

FIRST EDITION

ISBN   978-1-5445-3155-7   *Hardcover*
       978-1-5445-3154-0   *Paperback*
       978-1-5445-3156-4   *Ebook*

This book is dedicated to the girl I used to be.

Contents

Introduction

Have you ever been told to write a letter to your former self? I'm sure I've participated in this activity at least three times in my life. You're in some sort of religious lesson or girls' camp and the idea is that you write a letter to the girl you were a few years ago. You tell her all your wisdom and all the lessons you've learned. You encourage her to stick it out through the acne and the braces and assure her that eventually boys really do figure out what deodorant is. You tell her that she will eventually find a college major that she likes and not to worry because she won't end up pursuing a job in that field anyway. You make sure to mention that the argument you had with your sister isn't really that big of a deal in the grand scheme of things and to just let it go. You remind her of what is truly important and not to stress the small stuff. Had I been younger when social media blew up, I'm sure this is where I would've mentioned that the strangers I'd followed on Instagram were really the furthest thing from perfection, and that spending countless hours scrolling my feed was the biggest waste of time and brainpower.

I know I've completed this before. But I also know it has been at least a decade since I've done so. I paused the other day and wondered why. When did I stop seeing this as a useful solution to the problems I am facing? Retrospect is a powerful tool, one that not only puts past problems into perspective but also allows the brain to consider that perhaps the current issues are not as dire and earth-shattering as they may seem. So I told myself I might as well write a letter to the girl I used to be. And then, if I was going to write down all the lessons I've learned anyway, why not make it so that any girl could read it?

Why not publish it for the girl in her teens? Why not make it for the mom next door? Why not share it with my friend on Instagram? Why not write it to the girl who is a decade older than I am? Perhaps there are lessons I've learned along the course of my life that could help someone else. Perhaps there is something in the words that I will write that can touch the heart of another. Perhaps God could use me, just this once, to be a part of something greater than myself.

I've wanted to write a book since I was in elementary school. I even remember writing some version of a diary series when I was probably nine years old (think *Sweet Valley High* and *The Baby-Sitters Club* and you'll get the idea). As I grew up, my desire to write grew. I wanted to write a book—but not just *a* book. *The* book. A New York Times bestseller. One that would land me on *The Oprah Winfrey Show*. One that would get me on morning talk shows and make me famous. One that everyone would want to read. The older I got, the more detailed the vision became, and I just knew that one day, I was going to write a book.

The problem was I had no idea what to write about.

I racked my brain for years trying to come up with something to write about. I even started a book in college, but it just never seemed right. That was until a few years ago when I began looking back through my life and seeing the lessons that I've learned. That's when God told me what to write about. And, slow learner that I am, I am finally listening.

This book is a small glimpse of the shifts that I have made mentally and emotionally that have completely changed my life. They are the shifts that have led me closer to God and made me see Him work in my life in a very intimate way. They are the shifts that helped me forgive my husband after he confessed his secret pornography addiction. They are the shifts that helped me finally accept my body and (start to) love it exactly where it is. They are the shifts that helped me let go of resentment and bitterness in relationships. They are the shifts that have helped me see strangers with compassion. They are the shifts that have helped me see my past self with grace. They are the shifts that have helped me understand myself and others and see everyone as God sees us. They are the shifts that have helped me wake up and start living my life on purpose rather than simply existing in a monotonous pattern of contentment.

When my husband and I had been married about six years, he came to me one day and told me that he'd been secretly addicted to pornography for the entire time. Call me naïve, but it was not something I saw coming. There were no signs. No hints. No suggestions that this was happening and nothing in our relationship that would've pointed to this. It was as if my life had been flowing along freely and then abruptly hit a brick wall too massive for me to remove.

When he told me, I remember having two main reactions. The first followed the "fight" response instinct. Immediately I thought, "Okay. We can totally handle this." I began thinking of the next steps we could take to combat it. I wanted him to go to meetings, therapy, counseling, anything he was willing to do, and I was willing to shell out any amount of money to make that happen. (None of that actually happened for years because he followed his admission to me with the caveat of "I'm handling this. I don't need help, and I don't want to talk about it." All my carefully constructed plans to fight this thing head-on flew out the window and my "fight" response was left feeling utterly defeated. But that's a longer story for another book.)

My second reaction was much more subtle. It took me a number of years to even become truly aware of it. It was an internal retreat that followed the "flight" response instinct. I began to question everything about myself and our relationship, guided by the belief that there must be something wrong with *me*. Yes, I understood that his addiction to pornography was *his* problem…but he didn't even begin watching porn until after we were married. What did that say about me as a wife? As a sexual partner? What was wrong with me that would lead him to seek that out instead? What was I lacking that he sought out from other sources? **Why wasn't I enough?**

That question pounded within my subconscious for years. Buried deep. It was not a question I was comfortable with or even taught to believe. As a Christian who grew up in a strong, faithful household and church community, I was taught that I had worth. I recited scripture about my divine creation throughout my teenage years and intellectually understood that concept. But, until this point in my life, I never realized that I hadn't truly internalized it. I hadn't cemented that fully into my core. And because of that, I now found myself floundering under the belief that I wasn't enough. I wasn't skinny enough. I wasn't sexy enough. I wasn't a good enough wife. I wasn't pretty enough. I wasn't enough to keep my husband from watching porn. I wasn't enough of a reason to make him stop. I simply wasn't enough. I was the not-enough wife.

At least, I was for a time. But I didn't stay there for long.

Thanks to God's divine intervention and His grace in leading me along when I'm too lost to find my own way, I was led to discovering mindset and life coaching through podcasts. And I couldn't get enough. Here were the answers to all the questions I hadn't even known I had. Here were the tools I had never been given that were enabling me to put my emotional baggage to rest and move forward.

The more I healed, the more I let go, the more I began to move forward, and the more I felt compelled to share my journey with other women. I began to talk about my experience, and I became certified as a life coach to help other women who are struggling through similar situations. I became the life coach for the porn addict's wife. I started a podcast and launched my coaching business. And the more I began to coach, the more women I talked to, the more I realized something: most women, at one point or another, believe that we are not enough. Not good enough. Not smart enough. Not accomplished or generous enough. Not stay-at-home-mom enough or not work-from-home-mom enough. Not Instagram-ready enough or not do-it-yourself enough.

When I realized that, I once again felt compelled to share my journey with other women. Not just women in my same circumstances. But all women. Every woman who has felt that feeling of not being enough. I wanted to share what I'd learned with her. With you. And teach you to break up with that lie so that you can stop trying to prove to yourself or anyone else that you are worthy. To teach you that you are 100 percent worthy simply by the fact that you exist because God made you. You are not just the not-enough wife. You are so much more.

It was finally easy to decide what I wanted to write about.

In this book, I am going to teach you why so many of us believe this about ourselves, why it's so important to change it, and how to start changing it right away.

The things I offer you in this book are easy to digest. Applying them is what takes greater effort. Take what works for you and leave what doesn't. If you're willing to keep an open mind, I think this book could challenge your thoughts and hopefully create some of those same shifts that I experienced along the way. Women spend so much time fearing that they aren't enough. That they aren't doing enough. That they aren't strong enough, sexy enough, smart enough, good enough at their jobs or as a mom. That belief causes so much pain and frustration. But I know how to help change that. What I teach in this book will help you completely change the way you see yourself and help you show up in your life with more confidence and self-assurance than you ever thought possible. Bold promise, I know. But it's totally true.

I no longer have the same vision for this book that I did so many years ago. I don't care if it's a bestseller, and I don't think Oprah even does talk shows anymore. (Oprah, if you're reading this and you want me on your show, I'm in!) I no longer need the masses to approve (in fact, I'm pretty sure they won't). I no longer need fame and glory. My vision for this book has shifted so that it's no longer about me. Perhaps that's why it took me so long to finally write this. I needed to get my priorities in line. Because this book isn't for me. It's for you.

My story is not unique. And that's the power in it. It's not just my story. It's yours. All the pieces of our lives are beautifully woven together in an intricate web that connects us. So here are the pieces of my life, all laid out for you to pick apart and observe. If you learn a little something from it, don't thank me. Thank God. He's the one who made it all possible.

Xoxo,
Jolene

CHAPTER 1

You're more than just a number.

I remember being in physical science class in ninth grade. I was probably twelve. Yes, I was young for my grade, but before you get any ideas, it had nothing to do with my natural brilliance. It was all a tribute to my mother, who homeschooled me up until middle school, giving me the privilege of being in a class size of two. I can proudly claim I was the salutatorian of my elementary school. Of course, this also means I was the worst student in my school, but we'll just focus on the positive spin, shall we? In my ninth-grade physical science class, I remember doing an experiment that required a calculation of our weight. My teacher brought in a scale for all of us to use so that we could accurately record our weights into the equation. One by one, each student in the classroom weighed themselves and moved back to their seat to complete the assignment. I still remember what I weighed. 120 pounds (lbs). Naturally, as we began talking amongst ourselves, I heard my girlfriends share what the scale had read for them. 115 lbs…112 lbs…114 lbs…115 lbs…115 lbs…And suddenly, I was mortified.

I remember feeling completely embarrassed. Why did I weigh more than all of my friends? Why wasn't I as skinny as they were? Why didn't I look like them? It wasn't fair that I was heavier than everyone else in my class. Why did we have to participate in such an embarrassing activity anyway? Why couldn't I just be the same as the rest of the girls? I can still feel all that emotion as I sit here thinking back on it. I remember feeling ashamed and confused. I remember not wanting to share my weight with those around me because I knew that they would think the worst of me. I know that most of the girls reading this right now can relate.

Here's the craziest part of this story. I was never taught that my weight mattered. My mom didn't tell me I had to weigh a certain amount. My doctor told me that I was in the "healthy" zone. None of my friends told me I was too fat or too skinny. I was athletic and active, and every health class I'd ever had taught me that weight was simply the force of gravity on my body. Yet, here I was, standing in my ninth-grade classroom, when my brain started offering me thought after thought that I shouldn't be this way. I shouldn't weigh this much. I was too heavy. I shouldn't weigh five pounds more than my friends, *especially* since I was younger than them! I needed to start watching what I ate. I had to get this under control or I was going to just keep getting bigger and bigger…

Looking back, I can see that this had nothing to do with my education. Intellectually, I understood what the scale meant, and I understood that I was at a healthy weight for my height and age. But even "knowing" that, my brain didn't truly believe it. Instead, I believed that weighing five pounds more than my peers meant I was fat. It meant that I was too heavy. It meant that I was something that I shouldn't be. All these thoughts led me to feel embarrassed and ashamed. And I was twelve.

Here's the truth, ladies. Our brains are smart, but we are smarter. I'll say that again. **You are smarter than your brain.** Want to know why? Because you can choose your thoughts. Your brain offers you thousands of thoughts every day. But you can choose which ones you listen to. You can *choose* the thoughts that you allow yourself to think over and over. And if you don't like any of the thoughts your brain has to offer you, there is no rule that says you can't create new ones that you like better.

I started experimenting with this in college. I began to realize my obsession over the number on the scale was causing me anxiety and wasn't actually leading to any productive results. This was shocking to me. I truly expected that knowing my weight and keeping track of it would lead me to be more motivated in my eating habits and exercise. But you know what? It did the exact opposite. Instead of being motivated to progress and move forward, all it did was lead me to feel defeated if the number didn't change as much as I had hoped. I'd throw my hands up and say, "Forget it. This isn't working. I might as well eat an entire batch of cookie dough to make myself feel better." (Sound familiar?)

I don't remember when I figured this all out. It was sometime in college, perhaps even after I was married, when one day I thought to myself, "If weighing myself is causing me this much stress and anxiety, why am I even doing it?" (Insert mind-blown emoji person here.) This thought had *never* occurred to me before! Even though I hadn't considered my weight growing up, it was sometime around middle school that I began to notice and absorb ideas from society that my worth had something to do with my physique—which was largely determined by my weight.

Think about it: You go in for your annual physical at the doctor, and what do they do? They weigh you. You start working with a personal trainer, and what is the first thing they have you do? Step on a scale. We are taught over and over again throughout our lives that the best way to determine our level of fitness is by our weight, so my brain had simply never questioned it. Until one day it did.

Once I realized that I didn't have to weigh myself, I began to feel so much freedom. I suddenly felt motivated to track my progress in a different way: based on how fast I was running or how many reps I was lifting rather than the number on the scale. Instead of relying on my weight to determine my attitude toward my body, I reversed it and relied on my body to determine my attitude about my body. I began to feel motivated and empowered, and I began to see myself in a different light, one where my weight was irrelevant.

I'm blessed that I was able to grow up in a household and religion that taught me that I had an individual worth that was my birthright as a child of God. I grew up believing this with my whole heart. I never questioned it or doubted it or second-guessed it. I knew that God created me and that I had a divine spark inside of me. I still know it. And I believe it to be true for every human on this planet. But somehow along the way, my brain made my worth conditional. I kept thinking, "Yes, I know I am a child of God and have worth. But I still should weigh a little bit less. I still should be a little bit different." Do you see the danger in this? I had merged these two thoughts together to make my worth contingent on the alteration of my body. My brain had somehow convinced me that if I looked just a little different, if I were just a little bit skinnier, then I would be a more perfect daughter of God. I would be a better representation of Him and what He wanted in His children. My friends, *nothing* could be further from the truth.

My value as a woman didn't disintegrate because I didn't have a number attached to me. My individual worth didn't dissolve because I didn't know how much I weighed. My worth stayed *exactly* the same. Because

Your worth has nothing to do with how much you weigh.

Even though I grew up "knowing" this, I didn't fully believe it until I threw away the scale and realized it for myself. Until I had a new thought that questioned all the other thoughts that had been my foundation for measuring my health and fitness. Until I questioned the belief that my weight was somehow the determining factor of whether or not I was allowed to feel positive about myself.

After learning this, I had a few good years of positive thinking that helped me move forward and stay motivated even when I gained weight five times for five different pregnancies. (PS Losing baby weight is different than losing weight before you have kids. And it gets harder after every pregnancy—not impossible, just harder. Mamas, back me up on this.) I kept reminding myself that the scale didn't matter and that as long as I did everything I could to improve my health for that day, it was enough. That allowed me the perspective necessary to let weight loss take as long as it needed. Thinking the thought, "I am doing everything I can to take care of myself today" helped me keep focused even when my clothes still didn't fit or when I felt out of place in the free weight section of the gym. It is still a thought that helps me when I feel like I should be further along in my fitness journey than I am. But sometimes, my brain likes to go back to what it did the first few decades of my life and revert to negativity. My brain is comfortable thinking negative thoughts about my body. I have to be careful because even I can be tricked when my brain offers me thoughts that disrupt my newfound pattern of positive thought.

Allow me to give you an example. Just a few years ago, long after I had ditched the scale, I was feeling pretty pleased with myself. It was over a year after I had given birth to baby number three, and I had lost a significant amount of weight. I was thinking positive thoughts, not stressing about the scale (because I wasn't weighing myself), and feeling confident. Until my brain once again stepped in and started questioning the status quo. I started thinking thoughts like "Maybe I'm not progressing as much as I think I am because nobody has noticed…what if the reason nobody is complimenting me on my progression is that I don't look as good as I think I do…if only my husband would compliment me more, then I would feel more comfortable with what I look like."

My poor husband. Unbeknownst to him, I began calculating the time between his compliments and determined it was too long. I confronted him in an emotional mess of tears and told him that if he truly liked the way I looked, he should compliment me more, then I would feel better about myself. (Sorry, Rob!) Well, because I am married to the most wonderful man ever, he began to compliment me more, and do you know what happened? I still didn't believe him! Rather than thinking, "Oh, how sweet! My husband likes how I look and is noticing my progress and is attracted to me, and now I can feel positive about my body!" I started thinking, "Yeah, right. I had to ask him to tell me that. If he truly felt that way, he would've said it without me having to bring it up. Now he's just telling me this to make me feel better. Well, forget that. I'll just continue feeling miserable about myself even though he's doing exactly what I asked him to do."

Do y'all see the problem? I thought that it was my husband's job to make me feel good about myself. And it wasn't. Ladies, **nobody else can make you feel good about yourself.** Nothing outside of you can change the way you feel about yourself. Not the number on the scale, not the compliments from your spouse, not the size on the jeans you bought last year. It all comes from within. I thought throwing away the scale would change my feelings. I thought getting compliments would change my feelings. But do you know what changes your feelings? Your thoughts.

The thoughts I had in ninth grade made me feel ashamed and embarrassed. The thoughts I had through college made me feel anxious and stressed. And the thoughts I had in the earlier years of my marriage made me feel unattractive and resentful. Do you know what the common denominator is in all these situations and circumstances? You guessed it: my thoughts. You can throw away the scale, measure all your food, exercise daily, track your inches, buy new clothes, post progress photos, and lose every pound you've ever wanted to lose, but until you change your thoughts about yourself, your feelings will not change.

Think about it. Why do you even want to lose weight in the first place? Why do you even want to be a certain size or look a certain way? It's because you think that once you get there, once you achieve that goal, then you will feel a certain way. You think that once you are a size four, you'll feel confident. You think that if you had more curves, you would feel sexier. You think that if you had less acne and longer hair, you would feel pretty. You think that if your husband complimented you more, you would feel more attractive.

Well, guess what? That's not how it works. I thought not knowing how much I weighed would make me love my body, and it certainly helped...until my brain fixated on another negative thought. Then I thought that it if my husband said all the things I wanted him to say, I would feel more attractive...and guess what? It made me feel resentful and annoyed. You can change your haircut and buy new clothes and join a new gym and follow a million "inspiration" accounts on Instagram. You can learn how to contour makeup, wear false eyelashes, and do all the things you think will make you happy. But until you change your thoughts about yourself, none of that will work. Because trying to change our circumstances in order to change how we feel about ourselves does not work. Ever. And this is *great* news!

Because if how we feel about our bodies has absolutely nothing to do with anything outside of us, then we have all the control. And if attaining a certain goal is not what makes us feel better about ourselves, then we can feel exactly how we want right *now*. We don't have to wait! We don't have to wait until we are twenty pounds lighter. We don't have to wait until we get our braces removed. We don't have to wait until someone notices how hard we've worked. And we don't have to wait until we look a certain way to start accepting and loving ourselves exactly as we are right now.

I'm not suggesting that you simply say, "Excellent! I'll just tell myself I love myself every day, and then I'll feel better!" Because that's not it at all. You may be smarter than your brain, but your brain is not stupid. Don't underestimate it. If you begin telling your brain things like "I love my body" after you've been believing the thought "I hate my body" for the better part of a few decades, your brain is going to reject that. Immediately. Your brain knows that that is a lie, and it will tell you so right away. But if you train your brain to a more believable thought, I promise it can get there.

Again, let me illustrate with an example from my own life, shall I? After giving birth to baby number five in 2018, I avoided looking in the mirror for months. Literally. I would step out of the shower and studiously avoid the giant wall mirror that some contractor decided would be appropriately placed directly in front of the door of my shower (obviously a woman did not design my bathroom). I simply did not want to see the image of my body reflected back at me. Because anytime I did see it, I was mortified. It was like being in ninth grade all over again. My brain threw all those thoughts back in my face. Why do I look like this? Why can't I just lose the weight right away like so many other women? Why can't I just bounce back like everyone else seems to? Why does it take me so long to lose this weight?

I would feel ashamed. And then I would feel guilty because I knew that there were so many women who would gain one hundred pounds if they could have a baby, and here I was after giving birth for the fifth time to a beautiful, healthy little baby. I felt guilty because I was healthy, and I knew there were so many women who were sick and ailing and would give anything to be able to stand up on their own or exercise like I could. And that made me feel more ashamed.

It was around this time that I began listening to mindfulness and life coaching podcasts. I began learning about how our thoughts create our feelings, and it clicked with me right away. The more I listened and learned, the more aligned I felt with what I was being offered. I learned that my brain was smart but that I was smarter. This was a process of several months where I felt like I was waking up for the first time. I felt as if I'd been asleep my entire life and I was just coming to awareness of who I truly am and the potential that I have.

I learned that I could offer my brain thoughts instead of the other way around. I learned that I needed to come up with a thought that my brain would find believable. I knew there was no way I could go from a thought of disgust and self-pity to love and acceptance, but I did think it was possible to get to at least something neutral. I wasn't totally convinced that it would work in regard to my body image, but I was willing to experiment. I began stopping my brain when it would offer me the thought, "Ugh. Is this really what I look like?" Instead, I would force myself to look in the mirror and think "I have a body." Obviously it wasn't the most positive thought, but it was neutral and one that my brain was willing to accept. And it worked. For months I forced myself to look at my reflection and think the thought "I have a body."

What happened was nothing short of miraculous. Instead of feeling disgusted and ashamed and guilty and depressed like I felt when I had focused on all those previous thoughts, I began to feel grateful. I felt grateful for a body that could have babies. I felt grateful for a body that could exercise and move and function and allow me to participate in all the things I loved in my life. I felt grateful for lungs that worked and legs that ran and a smile that connected me to my kids. I felt grateful for a belly that carried five babies (even if that belly was bigger than I thought it should be), and I felt grateful for the thought that allowed me not to hate my own body.

I used that thought for months, and once I felt like it was more natural and took less focus and concentration, I moved on to another thought that was perhaps another slight step toward positive. I began trying on the thought "I am perfectly okay exactly where I am." This was harder because it required acceptance of my current physique rather than just a scientific acknowledgment of it, and, honestly, I'm still thinking this thought most days. It requires me to accept all the things I deem to be flaws, all the things that make me the most self-conscious, and to be okay if those things never change. And when I think the thought "I am perfectly okay," I feel more than gratitude. I feel peace and acceptance and love for myself.

Please don't misinterpret all of this as an excuse not to care for yourself. Your body is a gift, and it should be treated with respect and love. Self-love. And self-love does not mean neglecting your health. Self-love does not mean shaming those who are smaller than you or eating as much as you want for the rest of your life simply because you can convince your brain that you love yourself anyway. If you truly love yourself, you'll *want* to take care of your body in the best way you can. If you are truly comfortable with your body, you will *love* treating it with respect and giving yourself the grace to be exactly as you are, even as you journey to who you want to become.

I think one of the hardest things about body image is that our journeys all start and stop at different places and progress at different paces. Sometimes when we are on our journey, we look around, and our brain says, "Girl, get your act together. You should be *much* further along! Look at that girl—she's so much further than you!" I think this regularly about preteens these days. I look at all these middle school girls who know how to contour and get their eyebrows waxed, and I think, "Excuse me? Why does nobody have acne and wear their hair in a slicked-back ponytail? And how does this eleven-year-old know how to do her makeup better than me?" Seriously. Walk around Target and you'll know exactly what I'm talking about.

I especially struggle with this when it comes to losing baby weight. (Mind you, I'm nineteen months postpartum right now. Which is far enough along that you really can't claim it as postpartum anymore, but that's beside the point.) I'll be trucking along at the gym, feeling pretty good about my progress, and all of a sudden I'll meet some-one who is skinnier and only three months postpartum. Suddenly I'll feel all the self-loathing and judgment. It looks like this: "Okay, this is *not* fair. Why does that lady get to be all skinny and gorgeous right after her baby, and I have to go through *this*? In what universe is this fair? I'm going to have a serious talk with God about all of this when I get to heaven!" Suddenly, not only do I hate myself, but I also despise all the perfectly nice people around me. All because of my thoughts.

Comparison serves nobody. Period. All it does is create hostility and animosity when we could be creating encouragement. What if, instead of focusing on all the physical attributes that make us different from one another and seeing that as something negative, we made that something positive? What if we saw the girl who was more fit and, rather than being resentful, we applauded her efforts? What if we saw the girl who had gorgeously styled curls and, rather than being envious, we complimented her and asked her if she'd share her technique? What if we saw the girl with the body we think is "perfect" and, rather than assume she has everything figured out and loves herself, we asked her how *she* feels in her own skin and thereby helped her along her path? What if, instead of making all of this some sort of competitive race that only the lucky win, we saw it as an opportunity to create a community? Because, as women, we're all struggling with this. Every. Single. One. Of. Us. Once we realize that and embrace it, it allows us to see it not as "me" against "her" but as "us."

Here's the bottom line. If you aren't happy with who you are or the way you look or how your clothes fit you, it wouldn't matter if every other girl in the world were larger than you. You'd still be unhappy. The way anyone else looks in a swimsuit does not determine whether you have an enjoyable day at the pool. Your thoughts about how you think you look in a swimsuit do. The confident way women sit down at a table and converse has nothing to do with your discomfort about how your tummy rolls over the top button of the jeans that you should not have worn to a seated event. Your thoughts are what is making you uncomfortable. If you lined yourself up with a dozen other women who were all "bigger" than you and still felt uncomfortable with yourself, comparing your size to those around you wouldn't help your self-esteem.

> If you want to change how you feel about yourself, you have to start changing your thoughts.

My brain couldn't immediately go from hate to love in a day. And yours probably can't either. But that doesn't mean it can't happen. You can teach your brain to think anything you want about yourself, and there's nothing it can do about it. Recognizing that I could question all the thoughts that had created my self-image for two decades was powerful and helped me as I slowly moved forward.

I do want to emphasize just how slowly that was because it wasn't an overnight shift from depression to joy. It was a process. It *is* a process. I still have to remind myself that my weight simply doesn't matter. I still have to remind myself that I am more than a number. I still have to remind myself that it is nobody else's job to make me feel beautiful and confident (despite my wish that having my husband shower me with compliments would simply do the trick). And I still have to remind my brain to think the thought I want it to think rather than the other way around. But recognizing that **feeling positive about the way I look is entirely up to me** is one of the most empowering truths I've ever learned.

I didn't know all of this in ninth grade. I wish I had. It sure would've saved me a lot of stress about my acne and the size of my jeans. But I know it now, and I'm offering it to the girl I used to be, to the woman who has felt like she is somehow lacking, somehow not enough because of what she thinks about her body. Because if I could go back and show her all of this, I would. I would walk into that ninth-grade science class and give her a hug and teach her that she didn't have to listen to *any* of those negative thoughts. And neither do you.

You don't have to settle for thoughts that make you feel worthless and ashamed. You don't have to repeat thoughts in your mind that tarnish your value and make you second-guess your self-worth. You don't have to repeat thoughts over and over about how you should look or what the scale should say. And you certainly don't have to listen to thoughts that suggest that you are not good enough compared to the girl standing next to you. You are beautiful just as you are. And you are more than just a number.

CHAPTER 2

You were meant to be *you*.

I have an identical twin. Did y'all know this? Trust me, she's gorgeous. And talented. And creative. And successful. And kind. And everything I want to be when I grow up. From the time we were born (eight weeks early and a huge surprise to our mama—ask her for *that* story sometime for a good laugh) until we were about nine years old, we looked exactly alike. It's tricky to tell us apart in pictures, and usually I can only do it by looking for her earrings or the chicken pox scar on my forehead. As we grew up, we participated in most of the same activities and even shared the same strengths in academics (neither one of us can claim math as our greatest asset). We both played the piano, we both sang, we both played soccer and liked to read, and honestly the most defining difference between the two of us in our teenage years was that she played basketball and I was on the swim team.

You'd think that growing up with someone who looked a whole lot like you and did a whole lot of the same things as you would give you some sort of strange complex about not being as good as that person. Maybe for some twins it does. But rather than make me wish we were exactly the same, it made me appreciate all the subtle things that made us different. For example, she and I have never had the same sense of style. She is much more classic with a hint of trendy, and I am a hippie who loves to wear bell-bottoms and graphic tees. She loves conservative jewelry and traditional hair, and I think the bigger the earrings the better and have had every haircut and color under the sun. I love her style and can appreciate her fashion, but I truly don't want to dress exactly like her. I don't want to be her. I want to be me. And I can appreciate the preferences and traits that make us different.

The ability to observe differences without a judgmental comparison (either judgmental of yourself or the other person) is a skill, and it is one that I will spend the rest of my life developing. It is tricky to master because your brain is constantly offering you thoughts that pit you against other people. As women, we have become very good at listening to our brains when it comes to this. Somehow, we have allowed our brains to convince us that comparing ourselves to other women is how we are supposed to measure our own self-worth and success. But how backward is that? Why do we keep turning to other women, to outside sources, for the answer to our internal struggle?

The only way to determine who you are is by looking inside yourself. Nobody else can tell you who you should be. That is entirely up to you. Comparing yourself to the woman standing next to you, using *her* as the standard by which to measure yourself, is never going to get you the result you desire. Because *she* is not *you*. And thank goodness for that! Because the world would be a much less interesting place if we were all exactly the same.

Let me illustrate this with an example. My freshman year of college

I walked onto the campus and almost immediately felt the ugliest I had ever felt in my life. I attended a school where the girls were put together, fashion-forward, and it seemed like every girl I saw had flawless makeup and hair. It was quite a culture shock compared to the high school I attended where most kids wore sweats or pajamas and none of the girls got their hair professionally colored. Needless to say, I had a lot of feelings. Mostly negative ones. I felt frumpy and ill-suited to be around such beautiful people. I thought that there was no way that I would ever stand out to any guys compared to the girls I saw around me. I thought that because I didn't look like everyone else, I would be invisible. But instead it made me stand out.

My husband and I met that semester of my freshman year. The same year that I didn't know what Buckle brand jeans were or how to do makeup or do anything but straighten my hair. He says that one of the things he liked about me right away was that I was "real." He didn't just appreciate the things that made me different from other girls; he was drawn to me *because* of those things. He didn't need me to be just like everyone else. He needed me just to be me.

Now, don't get me wrong. I love myself some makeup and nice jeans. Getting my hair done is still one of my favorite things to do, and I love showcasing my personality with my clothes. And there is nothing wrong with that. But there *is* something wrong with doing the same thing as everyone else, wearing the same thing as everyone else, trying to be just like everyone else because you are uncomfortable with who *you* are on the inside. Pursuing the trends of the day because you like them and they resonate with you is completely different from pursuing them because you feel like you need to be the same as everyone else to be accepted and liked. The reasons behind your actions matter.

> Trying to blend in with the crowd is dangerous because you just might lose yourself there.

Where is it written that acknowledging the attributes of another girl must come at your own expense? Just because that girl is pretty doesn't make you ugly. Just because she is good at taking selfies doesn't mean that you should never take photos of yourself. Just because that girl you met once has beautiful teeth doesn't mean that your smile is any less radiant. Just because that woman you met at your husband's work party has a gorgeous figure doesn't mean that you are not attractive and sexy. Just because that girl can sing doesn't mean you don't have any talent. There's a thought out there that comparison gets you nowhere, but I disagree. Comparison sends you backward. It doesn't just halt your forward progress, it pushes you ten steps back.

This is a hard truth to remember. Especially when you are around a girl who is beautiful and embodies your personal definition of "ideal." You're feeling confident and put together, and then you run into a girl who is literally the living, breathing, human form of the word "perfect" from your personal dictionary. Suddenly, you're self-conscious and awkward, and your thoughts immediately spin to things like, "I am never going to look like her." And you're right. You never will look like her. Because **you are not her.**

Trust me, girl, I get it. We are constantly flooded with mixed messages that make us look to one another for clarification and direction. Be curvy but strong. Exercise regularly but don't obsess about it. Don't neglect any food groups and be well-balanced but don't overeat sweets and sugar. Be sexy but not to anyone but your spouse. Be confident but not proud. Be kind but don't be a doormat. Be healthy but not too skinny. Be well-groomed but not narcissistic. Be spiritual but not boastful. Be independent but don't forget to ask for help. I mean, I could keep going, but do I honestly need to? With all the directions we are being pulled these days, it's no wonder we are looking to those around us to see what on earth all of this means and *how* on earth we are supposed to be accomplishing it all!

It is completely natural to feel all of these societal pressures and simply freeze with the noise of it all. The conflicting messages tend to feed our insecurities about which direction to go. Having been there many times myself, I'll offer a simple piece of advice: **if you truly want to move forward, master the art of self-reflection.** Observing your past, present, and future self is the only form of comparison you will ever need. We spend so much time and energy focusing on those outside of ourselves, comparing ourselves to them, looking to them for some guidance and direction, but all the direction you need is inside of you. All the energy, all the focus, all the effort you put into observing others could instead be applied to your own beautiful soul. God has given you everything you need to figure out every problem you face. It's all inside you. Because He placed a small piece of Himself in your soul when He created you. And trust me when I tell you He's smarter than any woman on this planet will ever be.

So much of our lives are spent trying to mimic the actions of others because we don't know ourselves well enough to determine what we really like or are interested in. Isn't that fascinating? We mimic styles we don't like or that don't flatter our figures just because they're popular. We repeat phrases we don't understand and laugh at jokes we find offensive because otherwise we might not fit in. We claim beliefs and opinions that are not truly our own so we're not seen as close-minded. We expend hours of energy and tons of money to throw the perfect holiday party so that we appear chic and organized and social. We take up hiking because people in the area we live in seem to find that fulfilling. We shop at certain grocery stores, we date certain people, we buy certain toys, we style our hair a certain way, all in the attempt to conform to societal norms, even if we don't particularly like them.

What if we didn't? What if we looked into ourselves enough and knew ourselves well enough to only act when it was in accordance with our personal values and interests? What if we stopped looking around to everyone else to determine who we should be and instead looked inside us? What would happen? I'll tell you: the Earth does not explode. I know. Spoiler alert. It's true. And I'll tell you another secret, too: **if you start acting from an understanding and acceptance of who you are rather than simply following along with the crowd, you become yourself.** Let me show you what this looked like in my own life.

When I was growing up (with my gorgeous, fashion-forward identical twin), I hated shopping. Loathed it. But, being the supportive twin that I am, I followed along on many a shopping trip to the mall just for the social fun of it. I liked the atmosphere, I enjoyed hanging out with my friends, and I was pretty good at giving advice on what did or did not look good on someone. But I never wanted to try anything on, and I rarely purchased anything myself. Here's why: I didn't know what I liked. I didn't know that at the time. I thought it was because I wanted to save my money or because I had plenty of clothes at home. But as I have become better at self-reflection, I have discovered that it actually stemmed from the internal discomfort of not knowing what styles I did or did not like to wear.

I remember one shopping excursion very clearly. I was eleven or twelve, and I went to visit my grandma with my cousin on a special trip where only the two of us went. On this special trip, my grandma took my cousin and me to the mall so that we could each pick out an outfit—her treat. My cousin chose her outfit fairly quickly, but I wandered around completely lost. I felt anxious and overwhelmed, and I was so close to tears it was embarrassing. I just remember thinking "I don't know" over and over and over. My sweet grandma was so patient. She talked me through what I'm sure was a frustrating evening for her and took the time to help me find something to purchase. But I remember, even in that moment, wondering how I was supposed to buy an outfit when I had no idea what I liked to wear.

It took years of shopping and giving away clothes before I began to discover my personal sense of style. I discovered that I was secretly a hippie. I say secretly because it was a secret I kept from myself. I had to root that out and accept it. Once I embraced my internal love of bell-bottoms, floral print, and bohemian tops, I felt like a whole new woman. As it turns out, I actually love shopping. (Not that I get much traditional shopping done now because, as a mom of five, I'm just not interested in carting my brood to the mall while I try on clothes. As a result, most of my wardrobe is shipped to me via Amazon Prime.) I also discovered that I hate high-waisted jeans. I know that is not very modern of me, but there it is. I like low-rise jeans. I don't like flats, and I love high heels. I prefer gold jewelry to silver and wear wigs for fun. I *never* could have done this if I was still where I was when I was twelve—uncomfortable, anxious, and completely ignorant to who I truly am inside. I am a God-fearing, hippie mama with a rock and roll haircut living a traditional suburban life. And I love every minute of it because it is who I truly am.

If I hadn't taken the time to get to know this about myself, I still might be sitting in the JCPenney department store with my grandma, stressed and anxious about my life. I would be missing out on so many things that I find enjoyment in. I would be missing out on a piece of me that I can't even imagine being without now. And what's more, the people around me wouldn't really know me because I wouldn't be showing my true self to them. After all, **if you don't truly know yourself, how do you expect anyone else to get to know you?**

If you want connection, if you want love, if you want understanding, compassion, friendship, intimacy, and trust, you have to connect with yourself internally first. Without understanding yourself, you will never understand those around you. And don't get overwhelmed with the idea that you have a secret self hidden inside you that you have to go "discover." The truth is you can choose to be whoever you want to be. You have the freedom to choose. God gave that to you, and nobody can take that away. If you want to choose to be a hippie like me, more power to you. But if you don't really connect with that desire at your core, you won't feel like yourself.

Developing the art of self-reflection is one of the most powerful tools you can ever pursue. It not only allows you to accept who you truly are, it also allows you to recognize areas where you could benefit from improvement. You can never be too good at gracefully admitting that you are not yet the version of yourself that you'd like to be. There will be times when you feel like you've let yourself down, that you perhaps said something to someone that wasn't very kind, or you acted in a way that you feel ashamed admitting. I think these are the times when we are not acting as the people we truly are. This is not us acting and being our best selves. That's why we feel so ashamed and embarrassed about it.

But repeatedly beating ourselves up about it does nothing but make us feel more ashamed and more embarrassed. It doesn't propel us forward, and it doesn't improve us. So when you do something out of sync with who you truly are and with who you want to be, acknowledge it as not being your best self and give yourself the grace to accept it and move forward. Leave it in the past where it belongs.

Here's another truth about self-reflection. Once you realize that the way you are acting is not who you want to be, there is no law that says you can't change that. Right now. **Just because you acted that way once does not mean that you have to keep acting that way.** Did you know this? You can just decide to be a better person, a better version of yourself right now. Is it scary? Yes. Will people be confused and expect you to keep acting the way you have been up until this point? Yes. Will you possibly lose friends over it or be uncomfortable? Guaranteed. But what's worse? Being uncomfortable because you are pretending to be someone you're not? Or being uncomfortable because you are being the real you?

I've realized that I'm better at self-reflecting about things that happened in the past. I'm somehow much more aware of my failings and flaws, and I am much more willing to accept that I should improve. It is much harder to grant myself that same courtesy when I am dealing with a present struggle. I am much harsher toward myself, much more judgmental, and much more stubborn when it comes to change. Since I'm all about sharing as many embarrassing moments as I possibly can to y'all, I'll go ahead and pull an example from my own life.

I remember what I was like in seventh grade. Now, if you've ever been to seventh grade you know just how incredibly awkward it can be. It was my first year in public school (I had been homeschooled up until this point), and even though I was not any more socially awkward than any other seventh grader, I was just as desperate to make friends. I wanted to be liked. I wanted to fit in. Unfortunately, a number of my peers at the time were up to things that did not line up with my own personal values. In particular, there was one girl in my English class who encouraged me to erase incorrect answers on our spelling quizzes when we were asked to swap with a peer to grade. Suddenly, I was at a crossroads. What was I supposed to do? I knew cheating was wrong. But I also knew that this girl wanted to be my friend. And I had no idea how to tell her that I thought cheating was wrong. I ended up correcting her answers on many quizzes before my conscience got the better of me, and I told her I couldn't do that anymore. And guess what? She was still my friend. Imagine that. Here I had been worried all this time that she'd create a huge, dramatic scene and storm off, yet all she did was shrug and say, "Okay." Needless to say, it was not what I expected.

Don't worry, I went to my English teacher and told him the truth. I told him that I didn't deserve the grades I had been getting and that I would accept any consequences he thought appropriate. I was shocked when he smiled and thanked me for my honesty. Looking back on this experience, I can see myself with compassion for that little girl I was. I understand her confusion and desire to fit in. I feel gratitude for the teacher who was loving and gracious. And I feel proud that I was able to make a decision and act with integrity. Cheating was not me acting as my best self. It was not me showing up as I truly was. It was me being a phony, being false, portraying someone I wasn't. That experience taught me that **it is never worth it to act against your true self.**

If I could go back and teach my seventh-grade self that she didn't need to compromise her values in order to be liked, I would. I would tell her that she's enough just as she is. Unfortunately, Elon Musk hasn't invented time travel yet, so that's not an option. But I can do the next best thing. And that is to tell *you* what I would've told her. **You are enough just as you are. And you do not need to compromise who you are in order to fit in.**

As I mentioned earlier, it is easier to look at your past and evaluate your integrity than it is to do so with your present. I can easily look back at my seventh-grade self and evaluate where I had diverged from my true self. It's a much harder skill to do that right now. It's harder to take a look at yourself right where you are now, sitting in your room, in your car, in the middle of your life, and find out if you are acting as your best self. It takes curiosity and acceptance and a desire to improve. But it can absolutely be done!

Perhaps the best place to begin is by looking at your present self as if you are already who you want to be. What would you tell yourself if you were five years down the road? How would you approach the woman you are right now? What would you tell her? Would you tell her she's doing a great job as a mom and not to stress so much? Would you tell her that she will be so much happier if she stops trying to change herself into someone she's not? Zooming out can give you so much more perspective and give you the ability to see that who you are is truly enough.

You deserve to be the very best version of yourself, to be the type of girl who shows up for herself, to be the one who knows exactly who she is. You deserve to know what you like and what you don't like. You deserve to dress according to what you like to wear. You deserve to find friends who know who you really are underneath all the makeup. You deserve to live your life as you. Stop trying to be another character in your own story. Just be you.

Now, there is a fine line between being the real you with compassion and grace toward those around you and being the real you with an attitude and arrogance toward the world. I'll throw this out there in case anyone needs to hear it: you are not God's gift to the universe. That was Jesus. And even He didn't walk around with His nose up in the air at those who were beneath Him. He showed compassion, grace, mercy, and understanding. He knew exactly who He was, what His purpose was, and He never made apologies for it. But He never put anyone down either. He never used His kindness in manipulation, and He was never boastful or arrogant. I see so many women in our world today who think that being who they are means declaring their opinions without regard for others. It has exploded into a lack of common courtesy, a disregard for the opinions and feelings of others, and the adoption of a "take it or leave it" attitude.

To me, this is not what it means to be true to who you are.

> Being true to who you are is not meant to be at the expense of those around you.

In fact, you cannot be who you truly are without having compassion for those in your life. It doesn't mean you have to agree with everyone around you, but it does mean that you should accept that there are others with different opinions. If you believe that you get to be who you truly are, then those around you get to be who they truly are as well. The world is a much more beautiful place when we allow everyone to be who they are.

Imagine how much the world could change if we stopped pretending to be someone else. Imagine what it would be like if we shared our opinions respectfully and listened to others with curiosity rather than with judgment and disdain. Imagine if we actually knew who we were and were willing to act with integrity, even if that made us stand out from the crowd. Imagine if we were willing to discover our strengths and weaknesses, our passions and interests, our thoughts and beliefs, and then imagine if we were willing to act from those depths. Instead of constantly trying to be someone we are not or conform ourselves with thoughts and ideas that don't resonate with our core values, we can choose exactly who we want to be and act accordingly.

Once we realize that we have the power to do this, we are able to see that as a gift that every woman has. Even the nosy neighbor or the annoying woman in your spin class or the obnoxious younger sister or the crazy best friend. Every woman deserves to know who she is and be her true self. **Get to know yourself. I bet you'll like what you find.**

CHAPTER 3

Virtual "reality" does not exist.

Did y'all know this already? It's shocking to me how little we truly comprehend this, truly internalize this. Yet it is so sorely needed in today's world. The term "virtual reality" is a lie. Because anything virtual is *not* real because it only exists on the internet. And the internet is not real life. What *is* real are the people *behind* the screen. Behind the Instagram handle. That is what is real. Not the curated feed that is produced for your viewing pleasure.

In a world where we sit and consume what is right in front of our eyes, we begin to adopt the belief that what we *see* is what actually *is*. Our brains believe that the images we see, the videos on our feeds, the links on our platforms, are all the data we need to calculate an appropriate response and opinion about everything that is going on around us. Nothing could be further from the truth. Here's why.

Our brains have one job: to keep us alive. It's how we've evolved for centuries. Our brains want us to be part of the herd so that we don't get kicked out and left for dead like we would've been hundreds of years ago. But our brains can't know that we are actually able to survive quite nicely alone now. If we don't conform to everything we see, we will not die; we will simply be left out, which is not the same thing.

Unfortunately, our brains aren't smart enough to distinguish between "left for dead" and "left out" just yet. This is unfortunate because we are constantly flooding our brains with reasons why we should conform, why we should do exactly what everyone else is doing and that if we don't, we are in serious trouble of being left out—which our brains will interpret as being left for dead. So we sit on our screens, scrolling images and videos that tell our brains what we should look like, dress like, act like, think like. And this constant flood of information tricks our brains into believing that what we are sitting there consuming is, in fact, reality.

But **reality doesn't exist on a screen.** It never has, and it never will. Your favorite blogger shows you their highlight reel, your preferred news outlet targets their news based on viewer appreciation, and the ads that pop up on your Facebook feed are all based on your pattern of likes. What you see is not a full, complete representation of real life. It is simply a screenshot. It is a singular view that has been perfectly filtered to make you consume and keep consuming. No matter how much you consume, no matter how broad you attempt to make your searches, you will never get the complete picture online. Because it is not real life.

As a very old woman who was raised without a smartphone, I grew up with this knowledge. Having never had the benefit of smart feeds and 24/7 access to everything imaginable, I remember being wary and uncomfortable when it entered my life at the age of twenty-three. I remember being resistant to getting a smartphone because I had observed others getting sucked into the constant need to be watching a screen. I didn't want that to be me. Obviously, I succumbed to the pressure of FaceTiming Grandma and having the ability to take photos of my adorable six-month-old and later found the beauty of Instagram. I am in no way saying that all technology is bad; I am simply offering the idea that our brains are not biologically or evolutionarily designed to consume streams of content that are specifically designed to target our likes and influence our opinions. Not only do we adopt an unrealistic and untrue idea of "reality," we are also left vulnerable to the temptation to act differently in front of a screen versus in front of a real person.

Yet even with this knowledge, it took real-life application for me to truly see this and realize it as truth. My husband and I opened a small local business. A few months after opening, we had some local Facebook mom groups take exception to wording on our website and quite literally start a crusade against us. In the space of less than twelve hours, our business was slandered across multiple internet groups; we'd received dozens of hateful emails and direct messages; our business was torn apart with inaccurate reviews from individuals across the country who had never even been to our business; and women were taking it upon themselves to organize protests against our business. I was completely shocked. There hadn't even been an incident with a guest that people took exception to. It was a business policy that we'd written months before opening and never thought twice about. One visitor saw our policy online and took a screenshot, sharing it with an outside interest group, and suddenly we were the poster company for everything they disagreed with.

Having never been on the receiving end of cyberbullying before, it was an overwhelming experience. While I could appreciate their passion about the subject, what was the most fascinating to me was to see how these adults responded to their fervor. Rather than simply disagreeing with what we'd written or even asking us about it directly, women across the country made it their mission to destroy our business. And this is the crux of an incredible issue right now with social media and technology. The anonymity of a keyboard and the lack of consequences for digital aggression often encourage behavior in humans that wouldn't exist face to face. To more clearly boil it down: people forget that there are real people on the other side of their screen. Even as an adult and a life coach with all the emotional tools I have professional training in, it was still emotionally jarring. And, unfortunately, this is an all-too-common occurrence in our smartphone-centered world.

After this experience, I developed a heretofore untapped passion within me against cyberbullying. I don't use that term lightly. Before this happened with our business, I was more likely to say that people threw around the term "cyberbullying" too loosely, and that kids these days need to toughen up and get thicker skin or get off social media platforms. I stand corrected. This experience taught me that cyberbullying is a real and dangerous thing and that adults are just as much at fault as children, if not more so. The comments and messages I got from adults who had never met my husband or me were appalling. They were rude and hateful and spiteful to the nth degree. And this was all coming from adults. Adults who had been taught to be kind. Adults who would never say such things to another person if they were face to face. Adults who should understand how to speak to another human being without attacking them.

Suddenly I understood why cyberbullying is such an enormous problem these days. Because if adults can behave like this online, then of course kids are behaving just as badly. This problem isn't going to go away until we understand and teach our kids that screens are not excuses to treat people poorly. **While the virtual realm that we surround ourselves with is not the complete picture, that doesn't make the person on the other end of the screen any less real.**

The virtual world doesn't show us the complete picture of life, which is why it is false. It mainly portrays the best and the worst of the world around us: the best photos, the worst news, the best of humanity, the worst fails. Without all the middle, all the goings-on that happen in between the best and the worst, you miss the complete picture of what reality is. It's like you have a picture that only shows the edges, and the middle of the photo is completely missing. Without the middle of the photo, you can't even know what the photo is about. You may get an idea of it from what you see on the edges, but there is no grounding context. You will create your own story around what you see in order to explain it rather than taking it all in and observing it, absorbing it for what it is. Rather than seeing reality, you are simply creating a story about it in your own mind based on the fringes that you've been fed through a screen.

Let's look at this more specifically. What we see on social media is not an accurate representation of life because it is mainly the highlight reel of whomever you follow. For example, your favorite social media influencer, as forthcoming as they may be with their faults and struggles, is still an individual person with an agenda. They have a purpose behind their posts, and no matter how honest they are, I guarantee that the personal feed their grandma follows looks a whole lot different from the one that is curated and has thousands of followers.

Don't get me wrong, there is nothing wrong with this. But we have to tell our brains that what we are looking at is not the complete picture. Nobody's life is Instagram-worthy all of the time. That's just the edge of the picture. All the middle, all the messes, all the moments that we don't see are what complete the reality. The trouble is that our brains forget that. Our brains are incapable of seeing our social media feeds and making the deduction that what we are seeing isn't a true picture of reality. Our brains need *us* to be smarter than *they* are and to understand that **we are simply seeing the highlight reel.**

When you immerse yourself in a virtual world of make-believe, you forget that every single person's life is 50/50. Life is 50 percent negative and 50 percent positive for everyone. There is not a single human on this planet who has beaten those odds. Yet many of you would argue with me about this based on what you know of other peoples' lives. Based on the small screenshots and shares, headlines and headshots, you would claim that people exist who have somehow beaten this and come out with a much higher positive percentage. But the only reason you even think such things is because of the small scope you are able to see of their lives through your limited virtual connection. The mom next door doesn't have a life better than yours no matter what photos she posts on Facebook. And the influencer you follow doesn't have a better life just because her Instagram posts are positive and inspiring. Everyone has to deal with the negative in life. It's part of the deal. In fact, if we didn't have anything negative in our lives, we would never even understand that positive exists. It is the contrast that gives us enlightenment, allows us to grow, and allows us to compare and see our world for how it truly is.

The difficulty with this 50/50 concept is that individuals see others who don't have their exact same struggles and then assume the other person has no struggles at all. For example, to a girl who struggles with losing weight, she may see another woman's social media feed—see her beautiful, slender photos—and assume the other woman must be happier and live a better life simply because she doesn't struggle with weight. But perhaps the slenderer girl struggles with depression or addiction or has a terrible family situation that isn't shown through pretty pictures.

That's the falseness of the virtual world. It's only a portion of the picture. And the portion that gets shown most frequently on social media is the positive side. The side that is photo-worthy and ready. The side that is pretty and appealing and creates envy in the rest of us who engage with it. It's not the whole picture. It is only half. And it is our job to remind our brains of that.

In contrast to the social media world that tricks our brains into thinking that the world must be more than 50 percent positive for some people, there is the news that often tricks our brains into thinking that there must be more than 50 percent negative. Just as the world of social media tends to show us the highlight reel, our news feeds tend to show us the worst scenarios. The job of the news is to capture your attention so that you keep coming back for more. It is easier to do so with drama and fear than with news of goodness and peace. The brain is wired to keep us alive and will therefore stand captivated by negative articles and videos far longer than by positive ones that offer no threat. Your brain cannot differentiate between a virtual threat and a real one. That's why you can't seem to stop watching the news even when they are reporting something devastating or scary. Your brain wants you to keep watching because it is looking out for danger to keep you alive. But you are smarter than your own brain. You have to remind your brain that you are just fine, safe on the couch, where whatever is on the news cannot hurt you. The news wants you to watch. Your brain wants to keep you alive. When both the news and your brain are doing their jobs, it can be an overwhelmingly negative combination.

Now, please don't get me wrong. I'm not saying that all social media and news outlets are bad or evil. Of course they aren't. But I am saying that our brains were not designed to handle either of these as they presently exist in our universe. Therefore, it is up to us to recognize this and to remind our brains that while we may call it virtual "reality," it is more accurate to think of it as a special, curated feed that is more like a cropped photo. We don't always see the entire picture. And without the entire picture, without all of the details, we miss the full scope of reality.

I know this can seem overwhelming, but let's look at some practical ways to teach your brain how to handle what you see. The first thing you can do is edit your social media feed. How many influencers do you follow? How do you feel when you look at their feeds? Do you feel inadequate? Not skinny enough? Not pretty enough? Not stylish enough? If so, I invite you to simply unfollow them. The more you see the spectacular Pinterest birthday parties and magazine-worthy home shots, the more your brain will think that the "virtual reality" of what you are seeing is what your reality is supposed to look like. And that is not at all true.

This is important to remember, especially when we feel an over-whelming urge to keep up with appearances on social media. Spending hours scrolling through feeds full of impeccably deco-rated homes and perfectly coordinated outfits can offer our brains the suggestion that that is the "reality" of how we "should" be. This is where our brains start to gather information subconsciously that then dictates our ideas of what our own "reality" should look like.

For example, if I spend three or more hours a day looking at women on social media who are a size two with gorgeously styled hair, per-fect makeup, and clean homes, my brain is probably going to begin thinking that, if my own reality doesn't match what I am seeing, something is wrong. Our brains simply consume content that they then use against us. Our brains see the virtual world and have no understanding that it is not, in fact, reality. The expectations that a perfectly created feed put into our minds often lead us to think that our own messy realities are somehow lacking. That *we* are somehow lacking if we don't match the image on our screens. Our brains need to be reminded that what we are looking at is not a complete picture of real life. In fact, it is merely a virtual highlight reel that we are not meant to compete with.

It is no coincidence that cases of anxiety and depression have increased over the last decade with the development and explosion of social media. I'm not here to claim that all mental health struggles are a direct result of Facebook and Instagram, but I will tell you that it doesn't take a genius to see that they are connected. When your brain consumes information for hours a day that dictates an expectation, your brain will then compare what it sees on the screen to what it sees in real life. This comparison will typically find reality lacking because in no universe can the messy house, stinky diapers, acne, and piles of laundry be seen as better than the magazine-worthy woman on my Instagram feed. My brain will always come up with reasons why I am not matching what I see. Why my reality is not as good as the one on my screen. That creates the anxiety to do more, frustration with current surroundings, envy of others, and disappointment in ourselves.

I think the biggest example I see of this is in my comparison of my body to others. I love to lift weights and have been an avid follower of many fitness professionals for years. But I realized early on that I needed to be careful of the women I followed on social media. It didn't take long for my brain to think things like, "I wish my booty were bigger like hers" and "My stomach should be flat. Hers is flat. I want that." Even though I logically knew that these girls were never posting photos of themselves from a bad angle or when they felt bloated, it was still something that my brain used as a metric for comparison. And I always came up lacking. If you constantly compare yourself to your definition of perfection, your brain will always find the flaws in you, and you'll see yourself as not enough.

The secret to combating this tendency in our brains is to keep reminding your brain that what you are looking at is not, in fact, the standard by which to measure your worth. The virtual realm that we so often get sucked into is not what is real. What *is* real is human interaction. What *is* real is connection. What *is* real is the person on the other side of the screen, not the picture of them *on* the screen. What *is* real is looking into another person's eyes and actually seeing who they are, not just seeing the category our brain places them in.

When you are able to use social media and the virtual world to better connect with and understand the person on the other end of the Instagram handle or Facebook post, that is when the virtual realm and the real world mesh in a beautiful way. The people behind the screen are real. Don't get lost in the metrics and edited squares. Don't connect with the image that you see. Connect with the human behind it.

If you want more connection, more real interaction, look beyond your screen. Say hi to your neighbor and smile at the store clerk. Hug your kids and call your grandma.

> Your physical reality is so much deeper, so much more meaningful than a virtual realm—even with all the messes.

CHAPTER 4

Just because that's how *she* does it doesn't mean that's how *you* should do it.

Let me ask you something. Do you show up for each role in your life on purpose and with intention, or do you fulfill obligations and roles in a predictable way based on what you are "supposed" to do? My husband says that's a dense question, so allow me to rephrase. Do you do things because you want to or because that's what you've always done? Do you fill your life with things that you love or things that you feel like you should love? As a wife, do you have dinner prepared and ready most nights because that's what you like and find fulfilling or because that's what you're "supposed" to do? As a mama, do you discipline your kids based on your internal values or based on what you think you are "supposed" to do? Do you participate in hobbies based on your personal interests, or do you find yourself engaging in behaviors you have no interest in because that is what you are "supposed" to do?

If you've never truly thought about this before, it can be a bit murky. I get it. We are not very good at taking a look at our own expectations and why we have them; we are much better at asking ourselves if we are showing up based on someone else's expectations. So take a moment to truly think about the different roles in your life and evaluate how and why you fulfill each one the way you do. Of course, I'll now take this as an opportunity to divulge my life to you and illustrate with a few examples.

I hate cooking. I don't think it used to bother me too much, but once I started feeding the small army of little children that I had created, it became a nightmare. The planning, the prep, the cooking, the dishes, all for small children who hate everything anyway and would rather eat chicken nuggets. Add on the fact that my husband doesn't come home from work until close to 6:00 p.m. and the fact that the kids won't wait that long to eat dinner, and it basically means I ended up trying to cook dinner twice…a disaster. I loathed it with a very strong, fiery passion.

I'll be honest: I didn't cook that often. It's not like I was a gourmet chef who was preparing delicate, exquisite meals every night. But I was cooking more than I do now. And every time I made dinner, I was bitter and irritable. Every time I didn't make dinner, I felt immense guilt. I felt like I was letting down my husband. I felt like I was not fulfilling my duties as a wife. I felt like I was a failure, that my home was not what it should be, and that I should be a better wife.

Ridiculous, right? Yet that's how I felt. Because I thought that's what I was "supposed" to do. As a wife, as a mom, I was "supposed" to make dinner for my family every night. Even if I hated it. Even if it was hard. I thought I *should* make dinner because that's what a good wife does.

But who decides this? It's not like there is some code or book out there that you are presented with on the day of your marriage. You don't get handed a copy of *What Makes a Good Wife* after you say "I do" so that you can follow along with precise rules. It doesn't exist. We think it does, but it doesn't. **There is no code dictating your behavior. You get to choose exactly how you show up in every role in your life.**

The day I realized this was a glorious day. I still didn't make dinner. But I realized that I could stop beating myself up about it. Not cooking dinner for my husband doesn't make me a bad wife. (Insert mind-blown emoji here.) Did y'all know this?! Just because there are other wives out there who make dinner for their husbands every night does *not* mean that I am a terrible wife if I don't! Let that sink in and think about your own life. What are you feeling guilty about right now? Homeschooling your kids? *Not* homeschooling your kids? How many activities you do or do not participate in? Cooking dinner for your husband even though you hate it? Driving a certain car because other people at your stage of life drive that same kind of car? Pursuing a career in a certain area because that is what people your age are expected to do?

Take a moment and consider how you think you are supposed to show up in your own life. Why do you think this? Nobody handed you a manual at age thirteen and said, "Here's your guide to what you should do to be considered a woman." (In hindsight, I probably could've used that at age thirteen, but that's beside the point.) **There are no rules.** You don't have to be a size six in order to be a beautiful girl. You don't have to be at every birthday celebration in order to be a good grandmother. You don't have to be the PTA president in order to be a good mom.

Yet we think that all of these things are what we *should* do, and we run our lives based on the expectations and perceptions we have created inside our own minds. Just because there is a good wife out there somewhere who happens to be a fit, sexy size two does *not* mean that if I am not a fit, sexy size two, I must not be a good wife. Just because there is a good mom out there who goes to library story hour with her toddler and volunteers in her first grader's class does *not* mean that if I don't those things, I am not a good mom. Just because there is a smart girl out there who speaks two languages and plays the cello does *not* mean that if I don't do those things, I am not a smart girl.

Ladies, are you getting my point? Are you seeing how we do this to ourselves? We have each created internal manuals that dictate how we expect ourselves to show up and behave. We do this for each role that we have. Mom, daughter, teacher, sibling, friend, wife, sister, student…the list goes on. For every role and relationship you have in your life, you have created a manual that is running unconsciously in the back of your mind. And it may be causing you more stress than you think.

Let's take a look at another one of my personal examples, shall we? I used to run. Not quickly, mind you, but more than I do now. I would go for runs and train for a run here and there because I felt like that is what other stay-at-home moms did for exercise, so that's what I should do. To put it mildly, I didn't love it. I knew this. Yet I did it anyway because I had a little thought in my mind that that is what I should do as a stay-at-home mom. It was all because I didn't want to feel left out when other moms would say things like, "Let's all sign up for this run together! It'd be so fun!" So I would run and tell other moms that I ran, and I would feel a little bit like a liar and very self-conscious the entire time.

It took me years to become confident enough in myself that when other moms would decide to go on organized runs, I could simply say, "That sounds so fun! I'll come cheer for you!" and still feel included and loved. If you are filling your life with hobbies and interests that aren't your own because you feel like that is what you "should" do, you're going to wake up one day in a very unfulfilled life that doesn't feel like yours. What's the point in filling your life with what you think you "should" be doing if you lose yourself in the process?

Imagine this. It's like we have a filing cabinet for each role in our lives. Each role is labeled nicely and slid into place so that, in order to behave appropriately in all situations, all we have to do is pull out that file, look at the expected behaviors, and follow along accordingly. The tricky part is that we've been adding to each of these files subconsciously for years. Unbeknownst to ourselves, we determine appropriate behaviors, establish expectations, and file them in the correct categories so that we can whip them out to dictate our lives. Most of the time, this is a good thing. Most of the time, our file folders or manuals are filled with wonderful, positive things that benefit us. Things like "Moms should love their kids" and "Friends should be kind," etc. However, living life the way we think we are "supposed" to is very different from living our lives on purpose.

Allow me to differentiate. If you look in your "mom" file folder, you might see something like "Moms should love their kids." And following that expectation is not a bad idea. In fact, it's a great idea (and one I remind myself of frequently when my small humans are being particularly disobedient). However, if my folder also says, "Moms who love their kids take their kids to the park once a week" or "Moms who love their kids put them in music lessons at the age of five" or "Good moms only shop at these stores," and then I don't follow those exactly, I will end up making myself feel like a terrible mom who doesn't love her kids. It's all based on this tiny little manual I have running in my mind—one I didn't even know that I had. It just makes me feel guilty and worthless and doesn't serve me at all.

Let's do another example. If you look in the "wife" file folder, you might see something like "A good wife loves her husband." And that's positive and wonderful. You might also see "A good wife says yes every time her husband wants to have sex." This one is trickier because it *sounds* nice and positive and wonderful. It *sounds* like something that makes sense. It *sounds* like something that can only benefit and bring you closer together and be a great way to show love for your spouse. But, as I've seen with many of my clients, this actually leads to resentment, bitterness, and more distance in the marriage. In this case, the "wife" manual isn't serving anyone at all. And, more often than not, that's exactly what manuals do.

What manuals do you have for yourself? What do you expect yourself to do and not to do? How do you expect yourself to show up in each area of your life? Do you run because you're a stay-at-home mom and that's what you "should" do? Do you make dinner because you "should"? Do you have your kids in nine activities because you "should"? Do you stress about your weight because you "should" look a certain way? Do you work in a certain field because that's what you think you "should" be doing?

Just because you can do something doesn't mean you should.

Just because you *can* make dinner every night doesn't mean you have to. Just because you *can afford* to have your kids in every sport doesn't mean they have to. And just because your brain *suggested* that you could be a few sizes smaller than you are doesn't mean that you need to.

Let's say you're a stay-at-home mom. You start seeing all these other stay-at-home moms with "side hustles," and you think, "All these other moms have a side hustle. I should have one too." So you start teaching piano lessons. Maybe it doesn't start off so bad, but over time you get more students, it demands more time, it takes time away from your own kids, and maybe you begin to resent it and get frustrated. Maybe you hate that you have to do it after your husband is home and you get less time with him. Maybe you begin to hate it and wish that you weren't doing it because it's not financially necessary. But you keep going because you feel like you "should." Is that the life you want? Is that a reason to do the things you're doing?

Please, don't get me wrong. There is nothing wrong with side hustles or teaching piano lessons. My point is **there is a huge difference between acting based on subconscious expectations and intentionally choosing how you show up in your life.** It all revolves around how you feel. Two people can take the exact same actions and have entirely different results based on their manuals and their emotions. Let's take my example of making dinner. I expected myself to make dinner because it was written in my "wife" manual. My neighbor might have the exact same thing written in her "wife" manual. The difference is, for me, this led to guilt and anxiety. I felt like I "had" to complete this task or else I would not be worthy as a wife. In contrast, my neighbor could fulfill that task with joy and love and find it extremely satisfying. It's not the task itself that is the problem. It's how you look at it and what you're making it mean. For me, I was making the completion of these things mean that I was good enough. I thought that doing these things is what made me a good-enough wife. But if I could go back to my old self and tell that girl one thing, it would be that **doing things isn't what makes you good enough.** You don't have to prove your value and worth to yourself by fulfilling items on a checklist in your mind.

Now, you may be thinking, "Well, if I don't have a manual, how am I supposed to act? What's stopping me from just neglecting every responsibility in my life and doing whatever I want?" The answer is that, once you begin to recognize the manuals you have for yourself, you can start to take control over them. Instead of letting these subconscious programs run in the background, you can actually begin to *choose* the actions you take instead. This is where you start to decide what things you like and don't like, and find out why you behave certain ways and delete the behaviors you dislike. This is where you put yourself back in the driver's seat.

Don't worry. You're still a good person. And a good person will still be okay accepting responsibility. You'll still be okay with loving your kids and helping your mom. You'll still be okay with volunteering in your kid's class and coaching the soccer team. It just means that you can choose to complete those tasks out of love and joy rather than obligation and annoyance. It also means that you can let go of each of those things without being a terrible person. **You are a good person.** In fact, you'll be an even better one if you start acting with intention and purpose rather than out of subconscious programming.

This gets tough when our world is so small. We see all the other women on social media, in our neighborhoods, our churches, our work. "Susan makes cookies for her kids every weekend. I should do that too." "Jennifer exercises every morning before work. I am so lazy. I should be doing that." "Amy always looks so put together. I should really spend more time on myself." All those sneaky little thoughts are adding to your file folder every time you think them. But are they serving you? I'm going to go out on a limb here and say no. So start being aware of your brain. It's going to want to keep adding to that manual, that file folder so that it knows how to think and what to feel and how to behave. But remember: **you are smarter than your brain**. You already know how to think. You already know how you want to feel and show up in your life. And I'm pretty sure that you can figure out how to behave. **So stop listening to those sneaky little thoughts that add to your manuals.** You get to be you. And just because that's how *she* does it doesn't mean that's how *you* have to do it.

CHAPTER 5

Your brain is a lazy teenager.

My apologies to all the teenagers out there reading this book, but let's be honest, teenagers aren't always known for their productivity. Sure, they can be super productive in spurts. But given the option of sleeping in on a Saturday morning or doing chores, they're going to choose sleeping in most of the time. And your brain is exactly the same.

Your brain is an amazing machine, and its goal is to keep you alive. That's it. If you are alive at the end of the day, your brain thinks that it has done its job superbly. The way it does this is by running everything through a filter so it can decide which choice to make in any given scenario. This filter includes three things: What will produce the least amount of pain? What will require the least amount of effort? And what will give me the most pleasure? Those three filters (called the motivational triad) are how your brain determines every action it takes.

The reason our brains operate like this is because that is how they evolved to keep us alive. In caveman days, this is what helped us know that we should stay in the cave. Outside the cave was dangerous and scary and full of things that might attack us. Inside the cave was guarded and safe and kept us alive. To the brain, that's a job well done. The problem with this nowadays is that it prevents us from living a life that is full of what we actually desire. Instead, we end up living a life full of counterfeit pleasures and not understanding why we don't feel more fulfilled.

One of the three filters your brain uses to determine action is deciding what will take the least amount of effort. When you give your brain two options, your brain will make decision based on how little it must do to get the desired result. Once again, the comparison to the lazy teenager becomes more and more clear. For example, if your brain sees that you can earn a certain amount of money with or without going to college, it will probably argue against going to college because that requires more work. Another example is one I see in motherhood. If your brain thinks that all you need to do is keep your kids alive until the end of the day (no easy feat some days what with all the disobedience and the knock-knock jokes) and knows that can be accomplished either by being super productive or by lying on the couch, it will probably want to lie on the couch. Your brain prefers the path of least resistance. And it will lead you in that direction every time. This isn't a huge problem unless you actually *want* to go to college or *want* to be a mom who does more than sit on the couch all day. If that's the case, the brain being a lazy teenager gets in the way of you actually living the life you want to live. And it's important to become aware of that.

The next part of the motivational triad that cultivates decision-making in the brain is the part that wants to increase pleasure. This is a great way that our brains have evolved to keep us alive because it is what will motivate us to eat natural sugars, produce offspring, and create communities. However, it is also the part of the brain that can be tricked into thinking that concentrated, artificial pleasures are what we should pursue. For instance, the natural sugars that exist in fruit hit a center of the brain that makes it think, "This is delicious. Let's eat more of this." That worked really well until we developed artificial sugars that trigger that same physical response. This is why we have cravings for highly concentrated, artificial sugars. The part of the brain that wants to increase pleasure says, "This is delicious. Let's eat more of this." It doesn't understand that only eating artificial sugar isn't going to keep us alive and will instead give us diabetes.

Another example of this is pornography. Pornography is concentrated sex. When the brain sees pornography, it thinks, "This is pleasurable. We should seek this out again." It thinks that, because pornography triggers the pleasure part of the brain, it is something we should pursue. This is when learning how to become the boss of your brain becomes crucial. When we don't understand how to override the part of our brain that wants instant pleasure and immediate gratification, we can quickly find ourselves lost in a world of addiction to artificial pleasures. Once again, we find ourselves living a life where we are not the ones in control but are being driven by primal cravings we do not understand how to control.

Now, let's look at how your brain likes to avoid pain. This is perhaps the one that drives most of our day-to-day actions. For example, if you are sitting on the couch eating cookies, and you think, "I should probably go for a run," your brain says, "That's a terrible idea. Don't do that. That will hurt, and you will probably be self-conscious and slow anyway. Better to sit on the couch and keep watching Netflix.

Go ahead and press the button to watch the next episode." Why does it do this? Because it wants to avoid pain. Going for a run is usually painful in more ways than one. Not only will it be physically painful, it could also be emotionally painful. Your brain will think things like, "I should be faster" or "This is embarrassing," and you will then have to feel the emotional shame and embarrassment that go with it. Your brain wants to avoid all of that. It's much safer for your brain to keep you on the couch eating cookies, even if that's not going to get you very far in life in the long run.

The tricky thing about your brain operating this way is that, if you are alive, it thinks it can congratulate itself on a job well done. Even if you are alive in a life that you hate. Even if you are miserable. Or even if you're fairly content but there is more that you want to accomplish. Your brain wants to resist all of that and stay in what it knows. Why? Because what it knows is safe. What it knows is comfortable. The brain wants to stay in what is familiar. But what is familiar is not always what is best for you.

This is where knowing that you are smarter than your own brain can be super helpful. Because this is where you start to learn that **you are the boss of your brain.** Your brain likes to think it's in charge, but you just have to remind it that you are the one making the final decisions (just like a teenager might need reminding who is actually running the household, right?). Taking that Netflix and cookie example again, your brain wants to keep you on the couch because it's easier than putting in the effort to go for a run. But you have to be the boss and take charge. If you really want to do nothing else in your life but sit on a couch and eat cookies, then by all means, go ahead and listen to your brain. But if you don't actually want that, if you want a healthier body, then you have to tell your brain what to do. Even if it means some temporary discomfort.

Don't get me wrong, there are times and places where shows and cookies make the world a much better place. But if you allow your brain to run your life, you will wake up one day and realize that you are living a life far below your potential.

As humans, we like the feeling of comfort. We like calm and peace because it means we're safe. Our brains are wired to look for danger and keep us alive by avoiding uncomfortable or dangerous situations. Our brains like comfort because it means we can relax. It means our brains don't have to be on high alert and that we aren't going to die. This is why our brains like to perpetuate situations where we feel comfortable and avoid anything new or different.

We often face this most keenly when it's time to do something new and different. Our brains really like to freak out when we do this. Have you noticed? If you sign up for a new class or go to a new school or get ready for your first day on a new job, your brain will be losing its ever-loving mind. It has no idea what to expect, so it's a bit like watching a teenager try to get out of going to school. It will come up with *all* the reasons why it's not a good idea to do what you are about to do. What if nobody sits by me at lunch? What if my boss hates me? What if I say something dumb? What if I walk out of the bathroom with toilet paper on my shoe? All of the anxieties and fears of the unfamiliar come wafting up, and your brain wants to use them as a reason to go back to what you were doing before. But you are in charge of your brain. You can simply tell it that yes, you might feel some feelings today, but it's all okay—and you're going to do it anyway.

Now, I'm not just talking about feeling physically comfortable—lounging in yoga pants and watching a show. I'm talking about mental comfort. And emotional comfort. We feel this most when our lives are predictable. When there are patterns in place that we recognize and can predict and rely on. Patterns and predictability mean that the brain can relax, and that's what we're comfortable with. It's when those patterns get disrupted, and that predictability gets blown out of the water, that we experience discomfort and anxiety. This can happen if your loved one gets a scary medical diagnosis or if there's a worldwide pandemic or if your spouse comes to you one day and tells you he's been secretly addicted to pornography for your entire marriage. (All three of those have happened to me, and no, my brain didn't like it.) All of a sudden, the predictability is gone, and our brains go on high alert to look for danger and keep us alive. Suddenly, we feel anxious and uncomfortable.

Now, we think that the reason for our discomfort is because something is happening that we couldn't predict. But the truth is **we can never predict what's going to happen.** Ever. We've just accepted our realities and the possible dangers, and we have decided to be okay with that particular level of unpredictability and discomfort.

For example, my husband drives to work every day, and I'm comfortable with the predictability of him coming home just before 6:00 p.m. every night. (Okay, in full disclosure, he's a dentist, so he doesn't work on Fridays. But every night that he does work, this is the predictable pattern.) But the truth is I don't *know* that he's going to come home. He could get in a car accident on the way home one day. That is a realistic possibility. But I don't feel anxiety about it every day because my brain has accepted that possibility and has decided that that level of unknown, even if it's uncomfortable, won't kill me. My brain has gathered all the evidence and decided that my time is better spent not stressing about it every day because the odds of it happening, based on past experience, are slim.

Does this make sense? Our brains trick us into accepting certain discomforts that are part of our routines so that we don't change. Why? Because our brains would rather we sit with the devil we know than put forth the energy to change and face the devil we don't. Even though it's uncomfortable, it's a known discomfort. **Your brain will always choose the known discomfort over the unknown discomfort.** This is our comfort zone.

Let's do an example that most of us relate to. Weight loss. When you are overweight or not the size you want to be, it's not comfortable. Your jeans don't fit, you get out of breath walking up the stairs, you can't find anything to wear to church on Sundays, you stress about what your outfit should be for a girls' night out, and you feel self-conscious. You would think, with all of those discomforts, your brain would be inspired to take action, motivated to begin an exercise routine or change all your eating habits so that you don't have to have that discomfort in your life. But your brain is lazy. Losing weight comes with its own slew of discomforts. Getting up early, finding a gym, using equipment you have no idea how to use, putting on workout clothes, enduring sore muscles and aching body parts, feeling deprived of foods you crave, and feeling self-conscious. When your brain considers all the discomforts that would be involved in changing the status quo, it thinks those are too hard, are too painful, don't bring enough pleasure, and require too much effort. So it wants to stay where you are, in your comfort zone, with all the discomforts it already knows.

The problem with being comfortable is that we stay there. We are stagnant. There is no growth. No improvement. No progression. And progression and evolution are the whole reason we are here. We were created to progress. We were created to become. That kind of development only comes from being uncomfortable. Getting stronger requires the discomfort of resistance. **Moving forward requires facing the discomfort of the past head-on.**

I see this with clients who feel a lot of pain from the way someone else behaved toward them in the past. The unreconciled pain they cart around, the emotional baggage they carry, is uncomfortable and unpleasant to say the least. But it's part of their comfort zone. They are comfortable carrying that pain because their brains are fighting the alternative. Their brains don't want to face that pain and move past it. That is a discomfort that their brains resist. This is when they get to practice actually being the boss of their brains. This is where they tell their brains that they are going to face the discomfort head-on because their current comfort zone is no longer where they want to stay.

Allow me to illustrate with an example in my own life. Several years into working through and healing from my husband's pornography addiction, I realized that I was holding on to this tiny bit of hurt. Not a ton. Just a little bit. I was carrying around this pain from the past and I wasn't willing to release it. When I say it out loud, it sounds silly. I mean, who would choose to keep themselves in emotional pain, right?

Apparently, I did. Because the pain was familiar. The pain meant I was wronged. The pain meant that what he did wasn't right and he hurt me. Even though the pain was negative, it was comfortable. Familiar. And my brain really didn't want to get rid of it. My brain thought that getting rid of the pain would be more uncomfortable than just simply letting the pain stay there. My brain was afraid to let go of the pain because I'd held onto it for so long. Who was I if I didn't have that pain? What would that feel like? My brain was more scared of *that* discomfort than what I was currently experiencing. The truth is, I wasn't able to release the hurt and finally move forward until I was willing to embrace the discomfort of not knowing what came next.

The alternative to your comfort zone is growth *through* discomfort. If you look at the discomforts you are tolerating in your life, ask yourself this question: how different would my life look if I were willing to face the unknown discomforts that stand between who I am now and who I want to be? It's all possible.

> Question your comfort zone. The best version of you doesn't live there.

Now, this is easier said than done. I grant you that. Becoming the boss of your brain and getting it out of its comfortable routine is unpleasant. Much like waking up a teenager who doesn't want to be woken up. Your brain is going to whine and complain. It will list all the reasons that you shouldn't be taking action and give you a very reasonable-sounding argument for why you should stay exactly where you are. But you don't have to listen to it. **You are the boss of your brain. And you have bigger, better things to do that are waiting for you on the other side of your comfort zone.**

CHAPTER 6

There is no medal for being right.

My pride took a huge hit when I learned this lesson. And it took me years to learn. In fact, I'm still learning it. We get so wrapped up in being right. In doing the right thing, in being on the right side, in being the one who is right about whatever we are discussing. Yet what value is there to being right? And who decides it? And why do we spend so much time and energy on proving that we are, in fact, the one who is right? Why does that matter at all?

The answer is simple. Being right feels good.

That's it.

The brain likes to be right because it thinks that if it's right, that means it can stop working and relax. When it is right, it feels rewarded. Like it has done its job successfully and can congratulate itself and take a nap. The brain doesn't like to be wrong because then it feels questioned, unsure, as if perhaps there is something it may have missed. But here is a secret for you: being wrong won't kill you. You'll live. And, if you keep reading, you may learn that being wrong really isn't all that bad anyway since the only person who gets to decide if you're wrong is you.

Think about it. What if you just decided that being wrong was no big deal? What if you decided that being right was nothing to be proud of? What if, instead of spending so much of your energy and effort on making long Facebook posts to back up your righteous indignation, you simply allowed for the possibility that being right or wrong is irrelevant? I know that there are many people cringing at this right now, so bear with me for a moment.

What is the value of being right? What does that accomplish? Nothing but a feeling of pride within yourself. That's it. There is no award for it, no medal, no diploma. It simply generates a feeling within yourself that you find pleasing and wish to repeat. But it doesn't make you any more likely to succeed in life or make friends. In fact, the drive to always be right could do the exact opposite. Yet, as humans, we feel that it is our privilege to be right in most situations and to bring others to the realization of their wrongness. All to feel a little bit better about ourselves. However, my position is that **we can feel just as good about ourselves without fulfilling that compelling desire to be right.**

Feeling good about ourselves doesn't have to come from being right. If you truly felt that you were in the right, you would feel no pressure to argue others onto your side. Think about it. If you believed 100 percent in whatever position you were taking, you wouldn't feel the need to fight others to believe as you do. You would have compassion for them, understand their position, perhaps logically and calmly lay out your ideas, and let it end there. It is the desperation involved in proving yourself right that creates drama.

Being right is an intriguing concept because it also comes with the question of who gets to decide such a thing in the first place. As a Christian, I do believe in some moral truths and absolutes that I qualify as right and wrong, but apart from those, the only person who gets to decide if I am right or wrong is me. If I decide that swearing is wrong, then I am right, and others are wrong. If I decide that wearing shorts on Tuesdays is wrong, then I am right, and others are wrong. If I decide that plucking my eyebrows or playing video games or watching reality TV is the right thing to do, then that means that others are wrong. I get to choose what is right and wrong in my life. I get to decide if I am right or wrong.

Despite what the media suggests, there is no outside force or system that determines what constitutes right and wrong. We get to decide this for ourselves internally. We are not hauled before a court every day in order to see if the way we've styled our hair, written our name, or tied our shoelaces is the right way. Most of the time, it is simply our thoughts deciding if we are right. And we are in charge of our own thoughts.

Another intriguing thing about being right is that it automatically makes the opposing view wrong. Do you see how polarizing this is? If we constantly feel the desire to be "right," then that places us on one side of a conversation. It gives us a stance, a position. And it creates this need within us to defend ourselves and our decision. We are right. But we cannot be right without others being wrong. If there is a right and a wrong, then there are opposing sides. That creates the need to defend your position to the other person, which causes an argument. If you put yourself on defense, that creates an offense. Hence the universe we currently see. But if you just dropped the need to be right, what would happen? There would be no right or wrong, which would mean there are no sides. Without opposing sides, there is no argument. And without an argument, there is no fighting.

Now, I'm not saying that we should give up all of our values, morals, and guiding forces. Absolutely not. Please keep those. I'm simply suggesting that it is entirely possible to keep your moral rights and wrongs, even your opinions on all the other little things, and still leave a space between you and the world where you simply allow others to believe and be how they will be without creating tension about it.

Jesus was the best example of this. Of all the humans (or half humans in His case) that have ever been created, He perfected this. He was full of righteousness and truth. He knew what was right and wrong and, as the only one never to have sinned, He could for sure have acted pious and self-righteous because He truly was always right. But He didn't act that way. He managed to leave openness, space, and love between Himself and anyone He interacted with simply by dropping the compelling need to be seen as right. He overcame the pride of being right and was able to see that it is a false sense of position and recognition. He didn't only interact with those who were "right" in society or the ones who were acting like everyone else. He spent the majority of His time with those we would've considered beneath Him, showing them compassion and grace rather than pontificating Hebrew law to display His knowledge and spiritual prowess. He was still able to hold all of His standards and truths, never compromising them, yet discussed life with sinners and thieves, religious men who opposed Him, and political leaders who misunderstood Him.

Christ mastered this because He mastered His pride. Standing before Pilate, about to be crucified, He didn't start spouting all the ways that He was being treated unjustly. He didn't sit and argue about who was in the right and who was in the wrong. Instead, He stood with humility. Accepting the course even though it meant sacrificing not only His pride, but Himself. He was able to display compassion and understanding because He was willing to let go of His pride. And that is completely possible for us as well.

I learned about letting go of being right when my husband was addicted to pornography. We had been married for about five or six years when he came to me and confessed that he'd been secretly addicted to pornography since the first year of our marriage. I was completely shocked. I had never had any hints or indications that this was going on. And while I appreciated him coming to me about it, it was by no means the end of that journey. He continued to struggle with that addiction for several more years, and it was during those years that I began to become more aware of my thoughts and emotions, and how to process them in a healthy way.

As a Christian, I believe that pornography is wrong. Growing up as a member of the Church of Jesus Christ of Latter-day Saints, I was taught from a young age to avoid pornography. When my husband told me about his addiction, I very easily could've approached the entire situation believing that he was wrong and I was right. That would've been easy to spell out, and he would've agreed with me about all of it. But what would that have achieved? Nothing. All it would've done is put us on opposing sides—one where I was pointing out all his faults and failings, and one where he was feeling shame and guilt. When we are on opposing sides, it is impossible to work together to create a resolution. Being right solves absolutely nothing. By dropping my need to be seen as the one who was right,

I was able to allow enough space between us to work together and overcome his addiction.

Now, I don't bring up this story to highlight my own amazing attributes. I have plenty of sins, believe me. In fact, I think my own sins and failings are partly what helped me see this so clearly. Having done many wrong things in my life, I have needed Jesus just as much as my husband has. I have made many mistakes. But anytime I came to Jesus and confessed and repented and tried to be better, He didn't berate me. He offered grace. He looks on each of us with compassion, seeing us not just as what we do but as who we are. And that's what I was able to do with my husband. I was able to see him for who he is, not just the mistakes he made. That put us back on the same side, working together to fight against what could've very easily wedged us apart. That is what I want to offer here. Even in cases where what you believe is morally right and you are arguably *in* the right, coming into a conversation or relationship with that mentality doesn't typically produce a positive result. What is better is to try to hold space for compassion and understanding.

I see two main reasons that we like to hold on to being right. The most common one is that our brains often think that if we don't hold on to that rightness, we condone the behavior that we believe is wrong. Our brains get nervous that if we let go of a belief, that means what that person did wasn't wrong. That's not true at all. I struggled with this the most when I was learning how to forgive my husband. I wanted to let go of the pain and let it be a thing of the past, but my brain thought that letting it go meant that what he did was okay. My brain was afraid it would mean that I was fine with everything he did. It was a big internal struggle for me to work through. When I was finally willing to let all of my pain go, I found that the opposite is true. Trust me, being right is something I still struggle with because far too often, I believe I know best when I do not. But this story allows me to illustrate how you can keep your moral code of right and wrong and still drop the need to be "right." What holds many individuals back from letting go of their pride is the fear that letting go of it will lead to condoning behavior they disapprove of.

The second reason a lot of us hold on to being right is that we are often doing so to solidify our status. We are the ones who are the victims. We are the ones who know the truth. And we keep it that way in order to keep our story where we want it to be. This is why we are so good at holding grudges—it feels amazing. Holding grudges is simply holding on to being "right" and the other person being "wrong" in whatever scenario played out. Being "right" feels great because it is pride. But even though holding that grudge gives us a little surge of pride, it also keeps a wedge between us and the other person.

As I experienced in the example I just mentioned, holding on to my pride of being the one who was "wronged" in my marriage only created distance between us. I was elevated above him because he was the one doing the wrong thing. But as long as I saw us that way—with me as the victim and him as the villain—we could never truly come together and be on the same page to move forward. I had to accept that the pride I was feeling wasn't worth the result it was creating in my marriage. I had to be willing to let go of seeing myself as the one who was right for us to move forward.

Dropping my own need to be right and letting go of that last little bit of hurt within myself didn't make him right. And it didn't make me wrong. It made me free. What I learned from this experience is that the pride of being right comes with the cost of bitterness, resentment, and anger (with a side of a little self-righteousness). Those emotions are what prevent you from forgiving because forgiving is the absence of those emotions. Dropping the need to be right, being willing to let go of the bitterness, being willing to release the anger and resentment—that's what creates the space to forgive and move forward. I was so scared that the opposite of forgiveness was condoning. But I was wrong.

Forgiveness is the secret to your freedom.

When you understand why your brain likes to be right, it's much easier to realize how hollow that truly is. Because although feeling good about yourself is nice, although it feels good to keep yourself higher than others, although there's a worry that letting go of being right means condoning behavior you disapprove of, there are so many things that are so much better. Like understanding, compassion, love, and forgiveness. You cannot have any of those if you are insistent on keeping your "rightness" with you.

We often get so consumed with the idea that if you aren't right, you are wrong, we forget that's not true at all. We can give space for healing and opportunity for grace while allowing others to have a different opinion than we do without tearing them down. I know this is nothing like what we see today. The world today tells us that if we don't tear others down, we aren't truly standing up for our views. I disagree. Pride is what tells us that in order to defend our position, we have to attack. That's not the only option if you don't see being "wrong" as a terrible thing. Again, it goes back to who is deciding what is right and wrong in the first place—which is usually just you, in your own head.

One of the reasons our brains like to stay in the belief that things are either right or wrong is that it is easier to live a life without cognitive dissonance. Cognitive dissonance is when we have competing internal beliefs that create confusion and overwhelm. It is two conflicting thoughts that live in our heads. For example, I often see my clients struggle with conflicting thoughts because they love their husbands, but their husbands are addicted to porn, which they believe is wrong. Their brains have a difficult time reconciling how they could be in love with someone who does something they believe is wrong. Their brains then want them to choose one or the other. They should either be okay with their husband watching porn or reject their husband because he is doing something bad. This cognitive dissonance can be mentally exhausting because you constantly feel pulled in one direction or the other. This is why, as the wife of a man addicted to something you believe is morally wrong, you can feel completely overwhelmed and find it difficult to reconcile the man you love with the man who is doing something you disagree with.

The way to move through this without compromising your values is with acceptance. You have to begin by accepting that you are allowed to believe that pornography is wrong *and* that you can stay with him even if he continues to watch it. Our brain resists this because it is afraid that if we accept that he watches porn, it means we are okay with it. That's not true. But when you hold on to the label of "I'm right and he's wrong," you enter every conversation in opposition. Your brain automatically sees him as the other team, the one who is wrong, rather than as an individual.

I have seen this over and over again with my clients. When their brain insists on seeing their husband as wrong, he is always the bad guy. Not just with pornography but with the dishes, taking out the trash, and parenting. Learning that accepting people doesn't require relinquishing our hold on our moral absolutes and values can open up space in a conversation because we no longer show up as enemies and can instead come together as allies.

Our brains prefer that we simply believe there is a right and a wrong (and it likes to put us in the position of "right"). But this often leads to polarizing generalizations that don't produce anything but disagreements with those around us and refusal to compromise. We don't want to feel the discomfort of that internal confusion, so we avoid it by deciding that we are right and everything else is wrong. I think a very clear example of this is in political views. When we decide that we are voting a certain way, we often think that we are "right." Our choice is the best one and that makes the other one wrong. The problem with this is that, when we *need* to be "right," we attack the other side and place everyone who decided differently in a generalized category beneath us. Our brain thinks things like, "I am right and they are wrong" and enters every social media post with that angle.

But what if, instead, you simply thought of it as a decision? I made this choice, and they made that one. Do you feel how much more open that is? If we take control of our thoughts and acknowledge that, while there are cases of moral rights and wrongs, the majority of positions we take are simply decisions, we are able to come together in a way that facilitates discussion rather than argument. It fosters allowance and acceptance rather than judgment and fear. And that's when we are able to see others for who they are rather than simply for the thing they've decided that we think is "wrong."

Again, allow me to clarify that I do believe in moral absolutes. I don't believe we just have to get over the idea that murder is wrong and let murderers be who they are. That's not what I'm saying. But I am suggesting that you take this idea and apply it not only to the hundreds of insignificant arguments (such as the best movie ever or the worst date you've ever had) but also to the medium ones (like the best ways to discipline your child, how long you breastfeed, or whether or not you homeschool). And I am certainly suggesting you consider it for the big ones (like whether or not abortion is okay, if you stand for the national anthem, or whether or not vaping is a big deal in schools). If we were able to come to all of these discussions without this compelling need to be right, without the fear of being wrong, it would change the entire trajectory of the conversation. And we could do so without fear that dropping our need to be right would automatically mean the other side wins. Remember, letting go of that pride within ourselves doesn't make the other person right. It opens up the possibility for true communication.

There are no ceremonies for being right. There are no awards when you win an argument. You just feel a feeling. You feel a little rush of dopamine that you won, and you get a sense of satisfaction for proving the other side false. But it is a hollow victory. The pride you feel fades. And the opposition you created just leaves a bigger division between you and the world. **If we want a better world with less struggle and more understanding, we have to stop allowing our pride to drive the conversations.** Because there is no medal for being right.

CHAPTER 7

It's okay to cry.

As women, we are generally pretty good at crying. It is socially acceptable for us to do so in many instances (movies, baby showers, weddings, etc.), and we don't typically receive a lot of verbal backlash or bullying for it. You may be on the receiving end of some good-natured jests about being the one who always cries, but we are not taught that tears are a sign of weakness or that we shouldn't cry like men can be taught. However, I think that there are two types of tears, and we are really only good at showing one.

The first type of tears, the one I think we are fairly good at showing, is what I call socially acceptable tears. These are the ones that come out in socially acceptable situations (whatever we determine those to be). That could be during overwhelming scenes in a movie, while watching a daddy/daughter wedding dance, or during a funeral. Whatever our brains and our culture determine are socially acceptable times to show tears, that is when we are okay crying because we are comfortable enough to do so. For instance, if there were a group of women in a room where a brand-new baby was just born and someone started to cry, it would be seen as socially acceptable—the baby's birth would be interpreted as the cause for the tears.

The second type of tears, the one I think we are not as practiced at showing, is the socially awkward ones. The ones where it's not the situation itself that is presumed to be triggering the tears but rather an internal turmoil. This is when other people around you are completely unaware of the emotional struggle you are currently experiencing, and bursting into tears would not be understood by looking at the situation you are in. For example, if you are in a room full of strangers at a party and your anxiety builds to the point that you want nothing more than to start crying, you would not be looked at in the same way you would if you were crying over a birth. Nobody would understand *why* you are crying. (Which, of course, simply causes your anxiety to increase, thus making the suppression of tears even more difficult.) The pressure of that misunderstanding and potential judgment pushes us to hide our emotions even more.

I remember when I saw my mom cry the second way. Don't misunderstand—I saw my mom cry in socially acceptable ways *all* the time. My mom is a crier. She cries in all kinds of movies that most people would not think are emotionally charged and sheds tears over weddings, babies, and notes that I wrote in first grade. I saw her cry plenty. However, I do recall seeing her cry once when I didn't fully understand *why* she was crying. I was ten years old, and my mom was making dinner in the kitchen. She must've been upset because she yanked on the oven handle to pull the drawer open and jerked it in such a way that when she moved past it, she sliced a big hole in her jeans. She immediately put her hands up to her face, burst into tears, and told my older brother to take us younger kids out for pizza. I remember staring at her in confusion and being completely baffled by her response to the situation. Why on earth was she crying? It was no big deal, right?

As a child, I did not understand this. As an adult woman with five kids of my own, I completely get it. I have no idea what her day/month/year had been like, but I do know she was the mother of seven kids who were not always angels. She was almost always single-handedly running 397 different school functions and organizations. Not to mention the scheduling ridiculousness of nine lives, three cars, and a million activities. And that's all just what was on the outside. I have zero clue what kind of internal emotions and stresses she was feeling. So, yes, looking back, I get it. It was simply her reaching an emotional boiling point that I did not see coming and expressing it in front of me. Her response makes complete sense. But at the time it was confusing.

I understood it more when I became a mom myself. I distinctly remember my twenty-fifth birthday. I was supposed to have spent it with my twin sister, which would've required some shifting of schedules and traveling as we did not live near one another, but it didn't happen. I had an eighteen-month-old and a four-month-old, and though I can't remember all they had done that day, by the late afternoon I was overwhelmed. I sat on a chair, and I just started crying. My eighteen-month-old daughter climbed up on my lap and looked at me with the same confusion I am sure I had with my own mom, and she said, "Mommy sad." Her eyes were wide, and she touched my face as if she had no idea what was happening. It occurred to me that she had never seen me cry before. Ever. In that moment, I realized how important it was for her to see me cry. How important it was for her to learn that I feel emotions—not all of them pleasant—and that feeling them is completely okay. And that's exactly what I told her.

Even though it is generally more socially acceptable for women to show emotion, we still tend to resist it. We don't want to be over-dramatic or emotional. We want to be strong, capable, and resilient. The error lies in the belief that those are mutually exclusive—that being in touch with our emotions somehow makes us less capable, less resilient, and weak. This is a lie. **The more you can learn to be in touch with your emotions and process them, the stronger and more capable you will be.**

Think about it. How much of your life do you spend avoiding things because of how you feel when you experience them? How often do you skip social events because you don't want to feel anxious? How often do you avoid family dinners because you don't want to feel awkward? Do you avoid joining a gym because you feel uncomfortable there? Do you resist close relationships because you are afraid of feeling vulnerable? How much of your own life are you missing out on because you are trying to avoid a feeling? And what if you didn't have to live that way?

If you learned how to allow your emotions, even show them at times, your life would open up so much more. You would experience so much more. If you weren't afraid of your feelings, you would join that gym, attend that social function, reconnect with old friends, call your mom, write the book, go back to school…you could do it all. And that would be a much more full, complete life than one where you are trapped by your own emotion.

Consider this—which requires more emotional strength: avoiding your fear or facing it? (I'll pretend that you got this one right and move on.) Facing our fear requires us to harness that inner strength and resilience we are capable of, thus increasing our capacity to handle emotional turmoil. To put it more simply, allowing emotion makes us stronger. Avoiding emotion, pretending that we are not emotional creatures, holding back tears, all of those are simply a matter of hiding. And hiding builds no strength at all.

Perhaps a visual will help. When you lift weights, it's called resistance training. You build your strength by increasing the amount of weight you lift. If you stop lifting weights, your muscles will deplete. In fact, **resistance is required in order to increase strength.** We are *supposed* to feel emotions. All of them. Good ones, bad ones, negative, and positive. If we want to get stronger, we have to face the emotions we feel. We have to lift them, carry them, experience them. Avoiding them or resisting them is like dropping the weights. The longer you go without allowing that resistance to build your muscles, the weaker you become.

If you want to be a strong, capable woman, pick up the weights. Allow the emotions. Feel the feelings. Stop resisting them and pushing them away. Pretending not to cry doesn't make you stronger. It makes you weaker. Putting on a face doesn't make the emotion go away. It just shoves it down so that you carry it around to be dealt with later. The more you push it away, the weaker you get. When it finally comes back up to the surface (and it will), you'll be that much less equipped to deal with it. A fifteen-pound weight to someone who has never lifted before is a burden. But to someone who has been lifting for years, using resistance to build their muscles, that fifteen pounds is hardly noticeable. So it is with emotions. The more you resist emotion, the weaker your stamina to tolerate it. But the more you allow emotion in your life, the stronger and more resilient you become until even the heaviest of emotions are not beyond your ability to carry.

Now, let me clarify something here. Showing emotion or reacting to emotion is not the same as allowing it. This is a common mistake. We think that "allowing" ourselves to feel emotion is bad because it usually leads to fights, yelling, angry outbursts, uncontrollable sobbing, etc. But that is not allowing emotion. That is reacting *to* emotion. Allowing emotion is all internal. It is feeling the vibration of it in your body. Allowing it to be there. And still recognizing that you have a choice over how you will respond to it.

I know, this is getting a little woo-woo and hippie. Stay with me.

Have you ever simply sat and allowed yourself to feel? Have you ever sat and focused on what was happening inside your body? I think we all have moments of this, where we feel a lot of emotion inside of us and are aware of it. It could be when you feel nervous because you're about to perform a solo. Or it could be when you feel anxious because you are about to present in front of a group. It could be when you are about to meet your boyfriend's parents for the first time. Or it could be the love you feel when you hold your brand-new baby right after they are born. Those are times when we are very aware of the emotion we are feeling. We are connected to that emotion. We recognize it. We can identify it. We can experience it in a way we typically ignore. That is what I mean by allowing emotion.

Allowing emotion means you feel emotion without reacting to it or trying to change it.

Let me explain it a little bit more. Every emotion that we experience feels different in our bodies. Anxiety feels very different than grief. Fear feels very different than peace. Each emotion has a different physical manifestation that we experience. However, not all of these are very comfortable, so we resist feeling them. Usually, we turn to outside things in an attempt to negate the emotional discomfort. When we get anxious, we eat. When we get scared, we scroll on our phones. When we feel self-pity, we shop online and buy things we don't need. When we feel insecure, we gamble. When we feel lonely, we look at pornography.

When we don't know how to experience emotion inside our bodies, we try to make it go away or pretend it isn't there. It's why we have an entire society that is addicted to various substances and devices—we don't know how to feel our feelings, so we are constantly looking for distractions from them. The problem is that our emotions are always inside of us. The more we resist feeling them, the longer they stay inside us, which means the more we have to ignore them by consuming more things. It is a vicious cycle. However, we can break free from this cycle once we learn how to allow ourselves to feel our feelings and stop trying to resist or escape them.

Learning this tool is something that changed my life forever. My husband's pornography addiction brought up a lot of emotions that I would say qualify as uncomfortable. Gratefully, I naturally have a lower capacity to resist emotion; it simply isn't something I'm capable of. However, I still had to learn how to allow myself to sit and feel my feelings.

There was one weekend a few years ago that was particularly rough for me. I had just found out a few things about my husband's addiction that I hadn't known, and I was completely overwhelmed with worthlessness and rejection. I simply allowed myself to sit and feel it. Completely. For three days straight. I sat and allowed myself to feel rejected. I allowed myself to feel that hollow emptiness and sinking weight in my stomach. I allowed myself to feel consumed in darkness. And I didn't try to make it go away. I didn't try to distract myself.

Instead, I let it all be there. I let it be there as I sat on the floor of my closet and cried. I let it be there as I broke down and collapsed on my bathroom floor, physically unable to stand while I felt so consumed with the emotion I was feeling internally. I let it all be there. And it was exactly what I needed. I am stronger for having experienced it.

There's a false narrative in our society that our emotions are a problem that need to be fixed. Think about it: when children get upset, our instinct is to ask, "What's wrong?" so that we can fix it and make them stop crying. We've carried that into adulthood in a way that isn't serving us. What if there's nothing wrong with how we are feeling? What if it's exactly how we are supposed to be feeling? And what if we were okay with others feeling that way too? For example, I had a client come to me once and ask how she could help her daughter, who was feeling super anxious about something in school. I asked her, "What if you just let her feel anxious?" It was something she hadn't even considered as a possibility before. Why? Because we think that emotions need to be solved, fixed, taken away. That if we are feeling anxious, we need to make it stop. That if we are feeling upset, we need something to cheer us up. That if we are feeling uncomfortable, we should stop whatever we are doing that is creating that feeling.

But what if there's nothing wrong with feeling emotions? What if we are supposed to feel angry and scared and bitter and hurt? What if we can learn how to feel it without having to solve it? All of our emotions were created for us for a reason. We are supposed to feel them. God created our bodies so that we can experience every part of them, the good and bad, the light and dark, the opposites of every emotion. If we always felt happy, we would never know it because we'd have nothing to compare it to. Yet even knowing that, we are constantly trying to get back to that feeling of happiness, as if that's the goal in life. What if it isn't? What if the goal isn't to be happy all the time? What if the goal is to experience every emotion? If that's true, then feeling an emotion isn't something we have to fix. It's actually exactly what we need.

Think about this: if the point of life was only to feel positive things, then Jesus did it all wrong. Because He felt *all* of it. Way more than any of us will, I am sure. He felt joy and happiness and friendship, yes. But He also felt pain, heartache, grief, and loneliness. The point of life isn't to avoid all negative emotions. The point *is* to feel every emotion. Because that is what creates the human experience—the human experience that Jesus came to Earth to have.

Here's the truth: most of us are pretty terrible at feeling our feelings. But we are pretty exceptional at distracting ourselves from them. For example, what do you do when you feel anxious and stressed? Eat? Scroll through your social media feed? Binge Netflix? Shop online? We have very limited capability to feel our feelings, so when a negative emotion comes up, we immediately attempt to tune it out. Think about all the things we are addicted to nowadays: phones, TV shows, shopping, sugar, pornography, drugs…all of these are easy distractions that we use to avoid feeling our emotions. When was the last time you felt bored? It's hardly even a recognizable emotion any-more because we can simply turn our phones on and begin scrolling.

I know I am going to age myself here, but I didn't grow up with a cell phone. I remember spending a lot of time in the family van feeling incredibly bored while my mom ran errands. And do you know what? I survived. Because boredom is just an emotion. **And the very worst thing that can happen when you feel an emotion is you just feel it.** That's it. The world does not end, you don't die, you just feel the feeling.

What would your life look like if you simply learned how to feel your emotions instead of distracting yourself from them? How much more time would you have if you no longer gave in to the pull to binge Netflix when your kids went to bed and you didn't know what to do with all that pent-up anxiety from the entire day? How much more money would you have if you didn't compulsively spend your paycheck online to buy clothes in the hopes that they make you feel less self-conscious? How much more energy would you have if you stopped relying on concentrated sugar to get you through your bouts of anxiety? How much more freedom would you have if you didn't give in to the urge to drink alcohol or watch pornography when you felt lonely or stressed? There is so much *life* we miss out on simply because we are unable to feel our feelings.

If I were to write a letter to my former self, I would tell her it's okay to cry. It's okay to feel every emotion, good and bad. In fact, feeling emotion is exactly what we are designed to do as humans. It's okay to feel self-conscious. It's okay to feel sad. It's okay to feel excited and nervous and resentful and grateful. It's okay to feel compassion and hate and mortification and fear. Every emotion we feel is meant to be felt. Experienced. It's what makes our human life so incredibly powerful and bold.

I would tell her to stop trying to avoid emotion. Life is so much fuller with all emotions in it. Does it mean there will be more negative emotion felt? Sure. But there will also be so much more positive. When you understand that negative emotion is simply something you can feel and that it doesn't mean anything about you and that it is something you are supposed to feel, then it really isn't all that negative after all.

CHAPTER 8

You are not alone.

As the youngest of seven children, an identical twin, and a human being with a serious case of fear of missing out (FOMO), I am not often alone. At this point in my life, as the mother of five small children, being alone is actually a state that I aspire to achieve more than I try to avoid it. It is typically only accomplished at random bathroom breaks throughout the day and rarely for longer than two and a half minutes. However, being alone is a primal fear that all humans have and one that I want to address here today.

Let's begin with the reason we all find being alone so frightening. Evolutionarily speaking, our brains fear being alone because they think that being alone means that we have been rejected or ostracized from the group. Back in the days of cavemen and nomadic herds, being kicked out of the group meant you were left alone outside the haven of the herd to die. Our brains still haven't forgotten this primal fear and thus create a lot of drama around being left alone, even if there is not a real danger of death in most of our situations. This is why we want so badly to fit in. First within our family units, then within our friend groups in high school, and then in marriage as we get older.

My kids illustrate this fear when we are all walking out the door to go somewhere and everyone is rushing to put on shoes. My youngest two are always yelling out, "Don't leave without me, Mom!" (I still haven't figured out why they are so nervous about me leaving them alone in our front hallway with only one shoe on. It's not like that is a pattern of mine. I can only attribute it to this primal fear of being left out.) Children have a great desire to fit into their families and to be accepted by their siblings and parents.

Once kids get a little bit older, usually around middle school, fitting into the family becomes less important than fitting into a peer group. This is why kids will drop their traditional family values or behaviors and adopt what is "popular" among kids their own age. This fear of being left out, of being rejected, drives the desire to fit in. It's why they want the right pair of shoes, the smartphone everyone else gets, the ear piercing that all the girls are getting, the car that everyone else has. This fear overrides all the other considerations and is why some parents feel like their children become completely different people during these years. It's all because they don't want to feel left out, and they don't have the mental forethought to understand that what they are experiencing is temporary.

As adults, this fear is typically felt in the dating realm. (Can I just exclaim that I am oh so happy that I am no longer in the dating arena?) Dating is where all our fear comes right back to the surface. What if he doesn't text back? What if he doesn't like me? What if his family hates me? What if he doesn't want to date anymore? My husband felt this as a nineteen-year-old freshman in college right after we'd begun hanging out. (We weren't technically dating yet.) I had a terrible day on campus and called him to ask if he had time to talk. He said yes, so we met up. I had no idea of this at the time, but as I spewed and complained about my day, he was a ball of anxiety next to me. Apparently, he had interpreted my request for a conversation as a "we need to talk" exclamation. The poor boy sat there the entire time thinking I was about to dump him. (Which, again, would've been impossible seeing as how we weren't actually dating, but that's neither here nor there.) His fear of rejection, of being left out, of being kicked to the curb was creating a ball of nerves inside of him that didn't simmer down until I had finished ranting about my supposed troubles.

The fascinating thing about this fear is that we actually reach a point in our lives where we accept it as a possibility. This comes right along after the young adult dating phase. When you begin entering into relationships that are more substantial, you do so knowing that you might get hurt, that you might get rejected, that it might not work out, and that you might break up. And you do it anyway. The desire for connection overrides the fear of being rejected and alone. When you enter into a more steady, serious relationship, you do so knowing that it might not be "the one." This might not be the person you spend the rest of your life with. And, if that's the case, you might end with breaking up, which will lead you to feel rejected and alone. But you are willing to take the risk of feeling that emotion because the desire for connection and a true, lasting relationship overrides it. This is proof that **you can override the fear of being alone.**

Think about all the things you've done in your life simply because you were worried that if you didn't, you'd be left out. Perhaps you participated when you didn't really want to. Perhaps you sent a text that you wouldn't have sent otherwise. Perhaps you dated someone you knew wasn't great for you. Perhaps you joined a group, stayed friends with someone you didn't like, or married someone you aren't thrilled about. All because you didn't want to feel alone and rejected. But that's simply because your brain was afraid of feeling a feeling. Why? Because your brain doesn't know that **the worst thing that can happen when you feel a feeling is you just feel it.** That's it. Nothing else. The universe doesn't implode, you don't die, you don't dissolve. You just feel the feeling. And your brain is *so* scared of feeling that feeling it is willing to do all kinds of things you wouldn't otherwise do simply to avoid it.

When we feel an emotion, our brains want to make it mean something dire, something critical to our survival so that they can respond appropriately in order to save our lives. Therefore, when we feel an emotion, our brains will make it mean something more dramatic— and it may not necessarily be true. For example, if we are feeling loneliness, our brains want to make it mean that we *are* lonely. They take on that emotion as part of our identities, dramatizing it in an attempt to determine how to respond. But it's not necessary. And it's not true. When you feel loneliness, it doesn't mean you *are* lonely. It simply means that you are experiencing the emotion of loneliness.

This is an unfamiliar concept for most of us. It's not how we are typically taught to think about emotions, and it's certainly not how our brains think about emotions. But it's important to take into consideration because it allows us to experience our emotions without placing ourselves at the mercy of them. Recognizing that **we are not our emotions** enables us to create a space between who we are and what we are feeling. In that space, we create the power to experience emotion without being subject to it. **Your emotions are not in control of you.** You are in control of your emotions. They are simply something you are experiencing, even though your brain wants to make them mean something more.

I can acutely recall a time in my life when I felt alone. Not just lone-liness. But alone. (At least, that's what my brain told me at the time.) My husband was in dental school, and I had recently become preg-nant with our third baby. I immediately knew it was a girl. From the second I took that positive pregnancy test, I had a feeling that this was a baby girl. And I was elated. I told my husband, my twin sister, my two older sisters, my parents—it was something I was so thrilled about and was ready for 100 percent. Then, one morning I woke up early to exercise, and there was blood all over me. I was dumbfounded and completely in shock. Perhaps I had been naive, but miscarrying had never been something I considered before. Nobody in my family or my husband's family had miscarried at that point, and I had previously had two healthy pregnancies. My mind was simply unprepared for this. And it was rough. I tried to console myself with thoughts like, "It's okay. I wasn't that far along" and "This must mean that there was something wrong with the baby, and my body is taking care of it."

But it didn't work. I was still completely devastated. My sweet hus-band tried to console me by saying things like, "It's okay! We can try again as soon as you're able!" But that didn't work either. He didn't understand that I didn't want to talk about the next one. I wanted to talk about this one. This baby. And I wanted to feel sad. He didn't understand that. It was the first time in our marriage that I felt a distance between us. The first time that I felt truly alone.

With no one else to turn to, I turned to God. This was the moment in my life that I experienced Him as the Father He is. I had always known that He is my Father, always conceptually understood that and stood firm in that faith. But this was different. This was when I truly *felt* Him in that role. Not just as the Father of the world but as *my* Father. As a Father who weeps when I weep. As a Father who stands by my side when I have no one else. As a Father who loves and mourns with me in moments of sadness and heartache. It was in this small window of time that I came to understand that **we are never alone.** God is always with us. So in those moments of sadness, grief, pain, anguish, bitterness, disbelief, and despair, He is there. In those moments when we have no one else, when we feel most alone, He is with us. Sitting beside us in our lowest moments and darkest hours.

As God works in His own time and way, this first miscarriage of mine happened over Easter weekend. Even though it began with me feeling more alone than I had ever felt, that emotion was short-lived. The moment I realized that God was with me, I felt peace. I felt loved. I felt comforted. And even though I felt distant from my husband and felt the loss of my baby, I stopped feeling alone.

I think perhaps the reason we often feel so alone is that we have our eyes closed. Not only to God but to those around us. We close ourselves off from feeling connected with the ones who love us most. Think about it this way: it's like you are sitting on the floor of a dark room. Your knees are bent up to your chest, and your head is resting on your knees. Your face is buried in between your crossed arms as you face the floor. Your eyes are closed. In that position, even if you were in a room full of people, you would feel alone. Not because you *are* alone. But because you *feel* alone. Because you aren't seeing those who are next to you. Because you are closing yourself off from anyone else, everyone else. Removing the possibility that anyone could reach you. Denying yourself the opportunity to feel anything but alone.

This is something that happens in our brains called confirmation bias. When we believe something is true, our brains will look for evidence to prove it. The awesome thing about our brains is that they will always find proof that we are right, no matter what it is that we believe. So if you believe that you are alone, that nobody likes you, that you have no support, then your brain will prove it to you. It will collect evidence day after day, compiling a case so that you could prove to anyone who wanted to listen just how alone you truly are. But it's only doing that because that's the job you gave it to do. It would do the opposite job just as well. Let's say you are reading this right now, and you are arguing with me in your mind. You have years of evidence to prove that you are sitting in a room alone. That nobody is with you. That is true simply because that is the story you've been telling yourself. **You can choose to change your story.**

What if you stopped compiling evidence that you are alone? What if you stopped gathering proof that nobody likes you? What if you started to believe instead that there *are* people who want to be with you and help you? If you gave your brain the job of finding proof that you are *not* alone, it would find it.

I know that there are people reading this right now who are arguing with me in their brains. Saying things like, "Yeah, but I actually *don't* have anyone else. I actually *am* alone." What I want to offer is: that is never the case.

Even if there is no one else here on Earth that is with you, God always is.

When there is nobody else, He is there. Always. Even in times when we kind of wish He weren't. Times when we aren't at our best, when we are making mistakes, when we are acting against our own conscience, He is there. Sitting beside us. In the moments when we are struggling in our worthlessness, convinced that we are not enough, He is there, holding us. Helping us see how much of a lie that truly is.

I remember feeling this distinctly when I was working through the emotion of my husband's addiction. I had literally never felt more worthless. After all, as the wife, it was my responsibility to be sexy enough, appealing enough to keep him from watching porn, right? And, obviously, I had failed. (These are of course lies that my brain believed, but they felt very real at the time). I recall sitting on the bed in my guest room simply feeling the emotions in my body. Feeling the dark pit of emptiness that was rejection. Feeling the overwhelming weight of worthlessness I thought I'd never come out of. I felt oh so very alone.

Finally, I began to pray. I prayed to God to let me through this to the other side. As I closed my eyes, an image came to my mind. It played almost like a movie. I was standing in a large space with my husband right beside me. In front of us, lined up, were countless women. Gorgeous, incredible women. As I looked at each of these women, it was as if my husband looked back and forth between me and each woman and chose her over me. Over and over and over again. One by one. I know that's not actually how a pornography addiction works, but that's exactly how it felt. A punch to the gut and a little bit more feeling "not enough" with every woman we passed down the line.

I reached a point where I thought I couldn't take it anymore. I didn't want to feel this anymore. I didn't want him to choose them. I wanted him to choose me. I didn't want to feel like I wasn't enough for him. I wanted to feel like I was all he'd ever need. I didn't want to feel alone anymore. I prayed harder.

And that's when I turned and heard my name. And there, right next to me, was my Savior. He took my hand and said, "*I chose you.*" And, suddenly, all the weight was lifted. In that moment, I realized that I was never alone. Even in my darkest, heaviest moments. This thought that I am not enough is a lie. This thought that I am all by myself is a lie. I am enough for Him. And He is always with me. Just as you are always enough for Him, and He is always with you.

The world would try to convince us that we are all alone. Alone in our thoughts. Alone in our feelings. Alone in our pursuits and our struggles and our weaknesses. But that's not true at all. The truth is, even when we feel that we have been abandoned by the world, abandoned by our family or friends, we always have the God of the universe on our sides. He is waiting for us to turn our head and see Him standing right beside us. All we have to do is open our eyes to see Him. Because He is always there with us; we are never alone.

CHAPTER 9

Your identity is not determined by how you identify.

Have you ever introduced yourself to someone? The first question is typically "What's your name?" quickly followed by something along the lines of "So tell me about yourself" or "What do you do?" Answering the first question has never been a problem for me (except for the pronunciation of my married name…which is not what I use for my business dealings because it is difficult to pronounce and even more ridiculous to spell). My answer to the second question has evolved over the years. Allow me to illustrate.

It is fairly common that we identify who we are by whom we surround ourselves with—typically our families. In our culture, we even take our family name on from birth, giving us an individual identity but also a collective identity with those we are closest to. This is important for humans to once again avoid that feeling that we are being left out. If we had no cohesive unit to attach to, our sense of belonging and acceptance would not be as strong, and we would suffer emotionally as a result. (Think for a moment how emotional it can be for a child to be officially adopted and take on their new name, and you will see a clear illustration of just how powerful this can be.) As a child, I was a Winn. And that was how I told people who I was. That's how complete strangers knew a little about me.

As the youngest of seven, I spent a good decade at my older siblings' high school, helping my mom run the concession stand at football games, climbing an enormous dirt pile while my brothers played baseball, or setting up for After Prom and a slew of other activities. I was often around other adults who would look at me and ask, "Are you a Winn?" I would quickly respond in the affirmative, and that was all the identity I needed. They knew my mom, they knew my siblings, and so they knew a little bit about me simply from that identity.

As I grew up, my identity morphed a little bit more. As humans, we tend to do this. We identify ourselves not by who we are but by what we do. The activities we participate in, the hobbies we pursue in our spare time. It's one way that we make sure we stand out from the group as a whole, a way to make others know that even though we are a Winn, we are also our own person. Again, this is an illustration of that awkward time in middle school and high school when the family identity becomes less important than the peer identity. We want so badly to fit in to the crowd of insecure teenagers that we begin to identify more with the things that illustrate our individuality rather than our families. For example, as I navigated the awkwardness of the decade between ten and twenty years old, I began to answer the question "Who are you?" a little differently. Rather than emphasizing that I was a Winn, I began to answer with, "I'm a swimmer."

Swimming was a big part of my identity for years. I was an above-average swimmer, and I loved the sport immensely. I went to the state championship all four years of high school and was proud of my accomplishments in that sport. I began to take that on as part of my identity. It wasn't just what I did; it was a piece of who I was. It's very normal for teens and young adults (and even adults) to do this because it lets other people know a little bit more about you simply by hearing what it is you like to do. It's curious, though, to note that we often don't state it simply as an activity we enjoy—for instance saying, "I like to swim"—but make it a part of who we are—for instance, saying, "I am a swimmer." This is us taking on what we do and making it a part of our identities, claiming it as a part of ourselves. This is no problem in the moment. But what happens when you stop doing that thing you've used for so long to identify who you are? Suddenly you don't just lose something you did, you begin to question who you are.

Let's take an example. I identified myself as a swimmer for years. For much of my growing-up life, that was accurate. I swam every summer from the age of five to twelve and then swam competitively in middle and high school. But then I graduated high school. And I stopped swimming on a team. Suddenly I was no longer a swimmer. My brain couldn't quite compute that. If I'm not a swimmer, how do I tell people who I am? Who am I if I'm no longer a swimmer? How do I define myself to others and to myself?

I remember struggling to work through this my freshman year of college. I felt a little ridiculous telling people who I "used" to be. I solved this in two ways. The first was that I found a new way to identify myself by what I was doing at the time. I was a study-abroad student and a cadet in the Army ROTC program at my college. When I was introduced to others or was asked about myself and what I liked to do, I started sharing more of my current group identifications rather than those of my past. It took a bit of practice as I had been identifying who I was by my past activities for so long, but, over time, it became more comfortable.

The hardest part about this is that it requires an acceptance within yourself that you are no longer the person you defined yourself to be. Your brain struggles with this because it thinks that letting go of who you used to be means you are losing a piece of yourself. Your brain thinks it's almost like mourning a death, and perhaps in a way it is. It's letting go of your past self. But rather than allowing your brain to make it mean something bad, I want to offer that this could be the very best thing for you.

You now get a fresh start. A chance to completely reinvent yourself into someone better. Someone who is no longer tied to the decisions and labels you placed on yourself yesterday. This is a brand-new beginning. You have to learn to shed the labels of the past without making it mean that you are any less worthy or valuable. You have to learn how to see that *you* still exist, even if you let go of the old way of thinking of yourself. This just takes reminding your brain that you are who you are no matter what you do. Beginning new experiences doesn't mean the old ones didn't exist or make them any less meaningful.

No longer defining yourself by your past doesn't erase you. It frees you to begin a new chapter.

The second thing I began to do that helped me let go of my old definition of self was to learn more about who I was as an individual. Not just my skills and talents and group identities but my personality traits. I began to reflect on myself and basically did an internal inventory. (This wasn't an altogether pleasant process, as there was much about myself that I didn't want to acknowledge.) It was a process that took years, one that I am constantly undergoing as I strive to change who I am and become someone even better. I began to ask myself what I honestly liked and did not like about myself. And rather than using it as an excuse to beat myself up, I used that information to change.

I slowly realized that what we do on the outside is simply a reflection of who we are on the inside. If I wanted people to know me, I had to first get to know myself. Telling people what I did wasn't giving them the whole picture. It was up to me to share who I truly was, facing the fear that they may not accept it, but willing to do it anyway as that is what creates true connection.

A pretty clear example of this is what happens when moms become empty nesters. Most of us have seen some portrayal of this in our lives. Moms who have been identifying themselves by their children for the better part of several decades are suddenly without any child at home to tend. If they aren't primarily a mom anymore, who are they? The mental and emotional struggle this presents is based in the belief that who we are comes from what we do, the roles we take on in our lives. If those roles change, we no longer know who we are.

Not only do we think of who we are in terms of the roles we fill and the things we do, we also think of who we are in terms of the categories we place ourselves in. It's as if we go to something external to define who we are internally. We define ourselves by the group we associate with rather than having a definitive identity that we bring into the group. For instance, we define ourselves by our political affiliation, our skin color, our religion, even our generation. Especially in the last few years, popular culture places a huge emphasis on the categories we align with as being the most crucial pieces to our identities. The problem with this pattern of thinking is that it leads people, especially kids, to look outside of themselves to define who they are. **Who you are is not defined by what is outside of you or by what category you fit in to.**

For instance, popular culture today teaches that your sexuality is the most important piece of your identity. Social media and Hollywood push the narrative that your sexuality is not just a part of you but the crux of who you are. Hence the pressure to "find out" who you are by sexual exploration at an increasingly young age. Since most humans begin struggling with their individual identity in their middle school years, this emphasis on sexual identity thus promotes sexual promiscuity among children who are not even teenagers. If a person is struggling to understand who they are, and you teach them that the answer is in their sexuality, they will look to see how they compare with others sexually to determine their worth and value. Teen girls compare themselves to other girls on social media platforms, young adults compare themselves to Hollywood stars, and moms compare themselves to the neighbor next door to see how they are measuring up.

Ladies, we are especially good at this as we often see our bodies as a representation of our sexuality. We compare our bodies with the woman's next to us to see if we are "woman" enough. If we think we fall short, we feel ashamed for who we are. Add to this that you are constantly filtering in subconscious data from books and movies and life that add to that manual we talked about earlier, and you get a fully packed idea of what you are "supposed" to be. In our culture, you are a sexual creature that has codes to follow and expectations to keep.

The codes of our society for how women should be is a difficult balance of expectations. We are told to be sexy enough for our husbands but not so sexy that we attract unwanted attention. We are told to be proud of our bodies but not to display them in such a way that others notice too much. We are told that who we truly are is what is on the inside, yet we see stage after stage of girls in bikinis and wet T-shirt contests, telling us we are judged most on our bodies. We are told that we should be proud of our virtue, but if we don't sleep with a partner before marriage, we are called prudes. We are told that the most important thing we can do is be proud of our sexuality but not too loudly. Otherwise we'll be called promiscuous. As a woman, you should be able to keep your man satisfied at home, and if he's not, there might be something you're doing wrong. Bottom line, if you're a woman, you're expected to be exactly who society thinks you should be. Nothing more, nothing less. And if you don't measure up, then you've failed as a woman.

This hit me hard when my husband confessed his pornography addiction. Not only did I question my completeness as a woman, I took that one step further and questioned my individual worth and value. Because my brain had intertwined my sexuality with my personal identity so intimately, my initial response to my husband's addiction was to question my individual worth. In my brain, there was no difference between my husband rejecting me sexually and rejecting me as a person. They were one and the same. I felt rejected. Not just as a sexual partner but as my whole self. My brain just played this thought on repeat: I am not enough.

This is not an uncommon occurrence. In fact, in my experience, 100 percent of humans have this belief at their core: that they are not enough. The struggle then comes when we try to prove to ourselves that we are. We think that if we just *do* enough, *be* enough, that we will convince ourselves of our worth. It's why we try so badly to fit in somewhere. We are trying to resolve an internal sense of worthlessness with external praise. And it never quite fills the hole. We join clubs and groups, hoping that if we just work hard enough, we will be accepted. We take on the identity of the soccer mom, the PTA mom, the working mom, the employee, trying to embody that identity enough that it somehow generates internal acceptance of who we are. But **no amount of external acceptance will force internal acceptance.** We have to stop trying to solve this from the outside in and start solving it from the inside out.

The truth is you are not your sexuality. You are not your skin color. You are not your political affiliation or your achievements. You are not your education. You are not your hobbies. You are not the roles you fill or the expectations you place on yourself. You are not your skills or interests. You are not your body or your fears. You are not your insecurities or your family. You are not your name or your physical mannerisms. You are not your haircut or your wardrobe. You are not your actions or your mistakes. You are not your tattoos or your words. You are not your thoughts or your silence. You are not your feelings. You bring who you are *into* each of those things. You exist independent of those things. **If you took all of those away, you would still exist.**

The truth is **you are a soul created by God.** You are unique. You are loved. And you are 100 percent worthy simply because the God of the universe saw fit to create you. There is nothing you can do that will take that away from you. And nothing you do on Earth will fill you with acceptance like this knowledge. I think that, if people truly understood their worth and value, the true nature of their identity, they would have a lot less heartache. Truly knowing it, feeling it in your bones—not just believing it on paper—is what grants you the ability to come to know yourself. It's what enables you to bring who you are into the life that you live, rather than living a life in hopes that you will somehow find who you are along the way.

The key to accomplishing this, to truly coming to *know* who you are and understand your value and worth, is self-reflection. It's learning about your brain. Learning about your emotions. Learning how you think and feel and *why*. It takes deliberate effort and connecting yourself with your thoughts. And it takes purposeful pursuit. You aren't just going to come on this by accident. If that were true, a whole lot more of us wouldn't be struggling with our self-worth like we are. The best advice I can give is to start working on yourself. Read books. (Look! You're already doing it!!) Listen to podcasts. Hire a life coach—I happen to know a great one if you are in the market.

And don't forget to bring God along on the journey. Pray to Him. Attend church. Read His word. Put yourself in groups, spaces, and environments where this pursuit can thrive. Invest in your spiritual, emotional, and mental health just like you invest in your physical and intellectual health. It is going to be the best time, money, and effort you ever spend because, if you are willing to do the work, you will finally be able to see yourself as God sees you—as completely, wonderfully *enough*.

Your identity was determined from the moment you were created in the womb. And there's nothing you can do about it. No matter who you choose to identify with here on this Earth, it cannot override your eternal identity. Throughout your life it will be tempting to try and find out who you are. You'll join groups and take on roles that feel important and meaningful. And they are. But they don't make up who you are. You are not the college you attend or the major you choose. You are not the person you marry or the number of children you have. You are not the house you live in or the car you drive. You are not your job title or your résumé. You are not the image you portray on social media. You can fill your life with all of these amazing things, but they are not who you are.

You are who you are, and you bring yourself into those things. **Nothing has more value than the identity God gifted you with.** You are *His*. And because you are His, you don't need anything else. No other category. No other group. No other social movement or label. At your core, you are a child of God. And **you are always accepted as His.** With this knowledge, you are never lacking. You are never not-enough. God designed you from the beginning. **You are enough.**

CHAPTER 10

You are the author of your own story.

I'm rounding out this book with ten chapters so that my Grandma Holderness doesn't roll over in her grave. Her love for numbers and affinity for mathematics is not something that was passed down to me. (Although I did inherit her love for Dr. Pepper.) As I thought about how I wanted to end, this is what I came up with. And, yes, I know. It's a cliché chapter for a book. But listen up here, ladies, because this one is important. I know we "know" this. Intellectually, we understand that we are the ones who are in charge. But do you really get how crucial this is? Most of the time, we don't. Because we like to be the victims.

We like to think that the reason our lives are the way they are is because of things outside of our control. It's not our fault. It's because of other things. The family we are born into. The job we are stuck in. The consequences of others' actions that affect us. We think that we are unhappy because we can't lose weight. That we are unfulfilled because we don't have a side hustle. That we are lonely because our husbands won't talk to us when they get home. That we are distant from God because He hasn't answered our prayers lately. If only all of those things would change, then we would have the life that we've always dreamed of.

I have a secret for you: it's not true. Nothing outside of you is the reason you don't have the life you want. And this is the best news ever! Why? Because it means that **you don't have to wait for anything in your life to change to start creating the life of your dreams.**

This can be difficult to grasp, especially if you are living in a life that is affected by the consequences of another person's actions. I learned this in the years following my husband's confession of his pornography addiction. I spent several years trying to manage my future around what he was doing. And it consumed everything I did—what I wore, how much I weighed, whether or not I went on vacation, whether or not the house was picked up, how I disciplined my kids—it was all wrapped around his actions. I thought that my future, what happened to me, was directly tied to what he was doing. It took me a few years to learn that that wasn't true.

For example, I thought that the way I felt about my body was because he was watching porn. After all, my insecurities were manageable until his confession. Afterward, every time he touched me or kissed me, my brain went haywire wondering if he was comparing me to other women he'd seen or thinking that he must not like x, y, and z about my body and that I shouldn't blame him because neither did I. My brain was convinced that I felt the way I did *because* of his addiction. But it's not true.

The truth is my husband didn't create my physical insecurities. As we've discussed, I had those since I was in middle school. His addiction simply brought them to the surface. And this turned out to be the best thing ever for me. Because it made me realize that, if I created those insecurities myself and they weren't a consequence of my surroundings, that meant I could erase them. And that's exactly what I did. I realized that I didn't have to keep my insecurities around just because my husband was addicted to porn. I didn't have to use his addiction as an excuse to feel miserable about myself or hate my body. His actions didn't have to keep me stuck. That was something I was doing. And I could change it if I chose to do so. Was it difficult? Yes. But 100 percent doable.

This is why I can sit here today and write a book and say that I am actually grateful for my husband's pornography addiction. It gave me the opportunity to see myself in a brand-new way. To look at myself not as the victim of his actions but as the author of my own life. Sure, our lives are connected because we are married and I love him. But my internal story, my emotional health, and my mental happiness are not stories that he gets to write. He's not the author of my story. I am. And even though I was affected by his choices, his choices did not get to dictate my future. His actions didn't get to decide how I felt about myself or the decisions that I made. I was still 100 percent responsible for my emotional and mental well-being. Recognizing that completely changed my life.

I think one of the coolest things about what I do as a life coach is offer people possibility. Too often our brains will prevent us from moving forward simply because we listen to them. We aren't taught that we can question our brains. But you can. You can choose what happens next. Your brain might protest and say that it's too hard or that it's not possible. But it's wrong. Anything is possible. So ask yourself this question: if I could be anything I wanted, who would I be?

Now, I don't mean who would you be in a job or what career path would you choose. I mean, who would you be on the inside? How would you show up? Would you be confident? Trusting? Wise? Courteous? Generous? Free spirited? If anything were possible, who would you become?

Let that sink in for a moment. We are so used to letting other people write our stories. So used to having other people be the main characters. So used to waiting for the knight in shining armor to ride in and be the hero. So used to having a villain that is actively keeping us stuck. Yet none of it is true. **Nobody else is in charge of your story or what happens next in your life.** Unless that person is God. And even then, He often requires a little effort on our part. *You* are in charge of what happens next. You are the one who gets to create your future. You are the one writing your story.

One of the most powerful tools I teach my clients is that the life you live is the life you choose to see in your mind. We think that we simply experience life as it *is*. But the truth is that it's all how we interpret it. Everything that happens outside of us is a circumstance, and we get to choose how we think about it and react to it. This is how you can have two people experience the exact same thing and have two completely different opinions and feelings about it. It's because we get to choose what we tell ourselves about our lives. If we choose to see our lives as tragedies, they will be. If we choose to see our lives as miracles, they will be. It all comes down to the story we want to tell.

Think about it this way: if you were to write the story of your life today, how would you portray yourself? Would you be the villain or the hero? Maybe you'd portray yourself as the innocent bystander or the forgotten younger sister. Be honest. How do you see your role in your own life? Have you been an active participant, or have you simply gone through the motions with what is expected of you? If you were to write your story today, would you be happy with the ending?

The truth is no matter where you are in your story, it's not the end. No matter what has happened to you in your life, it doesn't have to define your future. You are in control. You are the one holding the pen.

> You are the one who gets to decide what happens next in your story.

And then comes the coolest part: you get to go make it happen.

This is one of the most underrated truths in life: **you get to create your future.** You can literally decide something and then make it happen. I'll give you an example. When my husband and I moved to where we live now, there were no indoor play spaces for kids. So we decided to make one ourselves. Months of research, late nights, meetings, and construction led to the installation of the indoor playhouses we'd purchased. As I watched this team of men install these custom playhouses, I became overwhelmed. Here was something we'd created in our minds suddenly realized. In that moment, I came to understand that **anything you think up can be created.** You just have to be willing to put in the work to make it happen.

It doesn't have to be as dramatic as opening up a brick-and-mortar business. It can be whatever you want your future to be like and whoever you want to be in your future. Whatever you want, you can make it happen. You can lose the weight. You can find the job. You can stop yelling at your kids. You can be comfortable in your own skin. You can conquer your anxiety. You can face your fears. You can create anything you want in your life. You just have to be willing to boss your brain around a bit to get there.

There is no limit to what you can accomplish. There is no limit to what you can achieve. There is nothing preventing you from having every single dream that you can imagine. And there is nothing so far out of reach that you cannot create it. You were made to be *you*. You were designed to live a full life. You have so much that God wants for you if only you can believe that it's possible.

So…now what? You've read a book and (hopefully) had a few new thoughts. How do you keep that going? How do you use the knowledge you've now gained and harness it in a way to actually create change in your life? It's harder than it seems. Why? Because your brain is lazy and doesn't want to change. That's why it puts off starting every new diet until the closest Monday. Changing requires effort. Staying the same is easier. Staying the same is comfortable. Your brain likes that. Your brain doesn't want you to change because changing requires more effort. Your brain is a lazy teenager who doesn't like to put in effort.

The truth is that the thing that comes next is whatever you want. If you want to change who you are, you can. If you want to change your profession, you can. If you want to lose the weight, start the job, join the group, begin the course, write the book, any of that is totally possible. But just as all of that is possible, it's also possible that you don't. That you don't take the action. That you stay exactly the same. That you don't allow this to change you. The direction you take next is entirely up to you.

Honestly, there's nothing stopping you. If you want to be free from a past trauma, it's possible. If you want to be confident in yourself, it's possible. If you want to be trusting of the spouse who lied to you, it's possible. If you want to be passionate, it's possible. All you have to do is decide. Choose on purpose. And then act in order to make it happen. Simple. Not easy, but simple.

So let me end with this: you get one life to live every day. A life that is entirely your own. A life that is created by you and determined by how you show up in it. So live it on purpose. Don't spend one more day believing that you aren't enough. Don't spend one more day hating your body. Don't spend one more minute wishing that you were not yourself. Because this world needs you exactly as you are. And you deserve to live a life where you become the very best version of yourself. Not because you are lacking, but because the world needs even *more* of you. Because you have always been enough. And you will always be enough. Watch your thoughts. Feel your feelings. Choose your actions on purpose and with the intention to create the life that you want to live. Allow God to move in you and direct you. Trust Him.

And go for it.

Acknowledgments

I'd like to thank God and Jesus Christ for leading me every step of the way. Even when I didn't see Them there.

About the Author

Jolene is a God-fearing, America-loving, rock 'n' roll hippie living a traditional suburban life. A typical day includes lifting weights at 6:00 a.m., raising five beautiful babies with her husband Rob, and helping women through *The Porn Addict's Wife* podcast and group coaching program she created.

www.jolenewinn.com

The Porn Addict's Wife podcast

@jolenewinncoaching